HAPPY DAYS

HAPPY DAYS
A thought for every day

Thora Hird
and Elizabeth Barr

HarperCollins*Publishers*

HarperCollins*Publishers*
77–85 Fulham Palace Road
Hammersmith, London W6 8JB

First published in Great Britain
in 1994 by HarperCollins*Religious*
1   3   5   7   9   10   8   6   4   2

A catalogue record for this book
is available from the British Library

ISBN 0 00 627802-7

Typeset by Harper Phototypesetters Limited
Northampton, England
Printed and bound in Great Britain by
HarperCollinsManufacturing Glasgow

CONTENTS

INTRODUCTION

I nearly always put 'Happy Days' before my name when giving an autograph, and as long ago as 1960 my dear friend, the late lamented Walter Greenwood, wrote a play of that name especially for me. *Happy Days* had its 'World Premiere' at the Coliseum in Oldham, followed by a season at The Grand, Blackpool — twice nightly and never an empty seat. (I hope you paid attention to that 'World Premiere' bit? Well, what's wrong with that? Walk tall, as they say!)

I don't think there could be a better title than *Happy Days*, because *Happy Days* exactly describes how Scottie and I feel about life. This little book is a 'thought' for every day of the year, and on some days I've included stories and memories of incidents from the past that have gone to make our family life so joyous . . . I'm not a 'holy Joe', but I don't think you have to be, do you, to love your family and want to count your blessings?

I hope this will be a book of thoughts suitable for every year, but I've been writing it through one particular year, 1993, and for us, as for everybody, there have inevitably been some not so happy days. We've shared with everyone the sadness of events unfolding in Bosnia; and we've grieved with the families in Warrington, and Northern Ireland, whose lives have been shattered by evil men.

If you're puzzled, when you read this book, when I talk about *Praise Be!* in the present tense, it's because at the beginning of 1993, while I was writing this, I was preparing and filming the seventeenth series of *Praise Be!* But, as you'll know, by the end of the year I'd received a letter from the new producer of *Songs of Praise* saying they wouldn't be wanting any more *Praise Be!* programmes. Now, you cannot know what pleasure the *Praise Be!* letters always gave me. Scottie will tell you, I would sit down every morning to read them, and answer all I could, but there were always too many for me to write back to them all. That was one reason why I started writing these little books in the first place — as a 'thank you' for the letters. They'll be what I'll miss — not the rest of it.

Please don't think this means I shan't be writing any more books. As soon as I have finished this one I shall be writing a second volume of my autobiography, because eighteen years have gone by since I wrote the first one, *Scene and Hird*, and I'm here to tell you, a lot of things have happened to us since then! I think I'll call the next one *Have you Hird!* What do you think?

Even as I sit here, putting the finishing

touches to this book before delivering it to the publisher, I've just had the great honour and pleasure of receiving the Variety Club of Great Britain Award, a big silver heart engraved in the middle with the words:

To Dame Thora Hird.
Special Award for Contribution
to Show Business.

That means a lot to me.

Now, I would love you to picture me rising in the morning, swathed in an elegant morning gown — do you call them 'peignoirs'? . . . sitting at a writing desk by a window — one overlooking a leafy London square perhaps — as I compose these great 'thoughts' on a pile of smooth cream-woven paper . . . But I have to confess that nothing could be further from the truth! My 'happy days', as often as not, begin with a trip round the house with the duster and hoover. And then there's the post to go through, scripts to read and lines to learn (with Scottie in the Prompt Corner). So my books are mainly written at top speed, travelling on trains, or between 'takes' when I'm filming, or in my lonely hotel room (boo-hoo — no Scottie — violins, please); scribbling away with a biro in an exercise book balanced on my lap, or on the back of old scripts and accounts ledgers. I then send them off to my friend, Liz Barr, who has always been my Right Hand Woman for seventeen years on *Praise Be!*, and who helps me put the stories together for my books. Otherwise, I don't believe they'd ever get finished!

I'm not complaining. I know that I'm a very fortunate woman, and I can honestly tell you, I never forget to be thankful that, in my eighties, I'm as busy as ever — busier sometimes . . . But I can still dream of life at that elegant lacquer-topped writing desk!

Well, here it is — a thought, a verse or a tale — for every day of the year. All 365 of 'em . . . I hope that for you as well as for me, they add up to a year of 'Happy Days!'

Thora Hird
Spring 1994

All Bible texts are from the Authorized Version unless noted otherwise.

JANUARY

If God sends us on stony paths,
he provides strong shoes.
Corrie Ten Boom

1 JANUARY

The sound of Big Ben chiming in the New Year at midnight — courtesy of the BBC — still 'gets' me, if you know what I mean. It sounds so majestic and full of portent. When Jan was living in America she would always telephone us at midnight, our time, to wish us a 'Happy New Year', but also — since she's every bit as daft as her mother — so that she could listen to Big Ben. Scottie and I would have to crouch on the floor holding the receiver close to the television set just so that Jan could hear that first 'Bong . . !' in Beverley Hills, and I used to whisper to Scottie, 'I say! I'm glad no one can see us!'

> But I struck one chord of music,
> Like the sound of a Great Amen.
> *Adelaide Ann Procter (1825–64)*
> *The Lost Chord*

2 JANUARY

I never fail to be amazed by how quickly after Christmas the things in our cottage garden seem to think spring has started! The birds are all singing their heads off in the mornings, as though it were at least April, and the frosty earth is breaking up to reveal the tips of daffodils.

3

I know we've still got a lot of cold winter days and weeks to get through before it's really spring — but all this excitement and energy of the birds and plants is catching, and I find I'm singing to myself today, as I dust and polish the cottage with renewed vigour before we return to London.

> I'll go
> In the strength of the Lord . . .

3 JANUARY

Our last day in the cottage before a dawn drive back to London tomorrow, where a frightening pile of post will be waiting for us.

We might go for a last walk today. Sometimes a strange, soft, muffled sound from the sky will make us look up, and there might be thirty or forty wild geese creaking their way over our heads. Their giant V shape looks like a huge arrow travelling slowly through the sky into the future.

I sometimes think Scottie and I live rather like wild geese — travelling backwards and forwards from one 'roost' to another!

> Lord, you made us for yourself, and
> our hearts are restless 'til they rest
> in thee.
>
> *St Augustine*

4 JANUARY
—‑—

Nobody seems to go back to work after Christmas before 3 or 4 January these days, do they? The Christmas break has stretched so much in my lifetime — from barely three days to nearly three weeks!

I sometimes wonder if everyone is really enjoying all this leisure in the middle of winter . . . It must be very lonely for old people on their own, when even the post office isn't open for them to go and get their pensions. They could have no one at all to talk to for a very long time.

I get letters on *Praise Be!* from people who once belonged to big, happy families and are now so alone, and it upsets me very much. I'm not someone who enjoys their own company, so I always try to remember to say special prayers for anyone spending these cold days on their own.

> O God, thou hast taught me from
> my youth: and hitherto have I
> declared thy wondrous works.
> Now also when I am old and grey-
> headed, O God, forsake me not . . .
> *Psalm 71:17–18*

5 JANUARY

--

One of the best writers and broadcasters about the Christian life that I've ever come across was Dr William Barclay, Professor of Divinity and Biblical Criticism at Glasgow University, who died in January 1978. He wrote a wonderful series of books which he called 'The Plain Man's Guides'.

In the dark days of winter, if you're like me, you may be finding the long nights and short, bitter days rather wearing. Try saying one of William Barclay's prayers for the Plain Man:

> O God, somehow nowadays I am
> always tired. I go to sleep tired and
> I get up still tired.
> Things take longer than they used
> to take, and I get behind with my
> work, and with the things I ought
> to do. I come home tired, and that
> makes me cross and bad-tempered
> and irritable and impatient with my
> own family and my own people.
> Everything has become an effort
> and a labour.
> O God, help me to keep going, and
> help me to find something of the
> rest which you alone can give.
> Refresh me with your presence, and
> give me back the joy of living and

the thrill of working: through Jesus
Christ my Lord. Amen.

William Barclay (1907–78)
More Prayers for the Plain Man

6 JANUARY

Epiphany

Twelfth Night, and at last I can take down all
the decorations and cards, and have a good 'go'
round the house with a duster and polish — my
way of celebrating the arrival of the Three Wise
Men! The Eastern Orthodox churches keep to
the oldest Christian calendar, so for them it's
Christmas Eve today.

> And when they were come into the
> house, they saw the young child
> with Mary his mother, and fell
> down, and worshipped him: and
> when they had opened their
> treasures, they presented unto him
> gifts; gold, and frankincense, and
> myrrh.
>
> *Matthew 2:11*

7

7 JANUARY

The Revd Roger Dalling, our vicar, is a magician! That's the only word for it. Some evenings we have services in our ancient parish church lit only by the candles on the altar, and there's always the sort of attentive silence that an actor would give anything for, as Roger leads a group of us in night-time prayers for the world.

At other times, in the mornings, there will be crowds there, and the little church is transformed by light and colour and noise, with processions of children, and stories — the old Christian stories — but told so you feel it has all just happened . . . very recently . . . and somewhere very near.

> Yet in thy dark streets shineth
> The everlasting Light;
> The hopes and fears of all the years
> Are met in thee tonight.
> *Phillips Brooks (1835–93)*
> *'O little town of Bethlehem'*

8 JANUARY

I'll never forget one year on the first Sunday after the Epiphany, Roger told us all to imagine the last part of the journey of the Wise Men. Well, he was speaking to the children, really, but we were *all* spellbound. He said Bethlehem is about as far from Jerusalem as Lewes, our county town, is from our village. He said we were to imagine riding camels across the South Downs, and finding the baby Jesus in the car-park at the back of the inn — our inn — the Laughing Fish!

Wise Men Seeking Jesus
Wise men seeking Jesus,
Travelled from afar,
Guided on their journey
By a beauteous star.

But if we desire him,
He is close at hand;
For our native country
Is our Holy Land.

Prayerful souls may find him
By our quiet lakes,
Meet him on our hillsides
When the morning breaks.
James Thomas East (1860–1937)

9 JANUARY

Wise Men Seeking Jesus was written by a Methodist minister, James East, because he had always dreamed of making a pilgrimage to the Holy Land, but every year something always prevented him from going. The day came when he realized that he would *never* be going, and that day he sat down to write the words of his wonderful Epiphany hymn.

(Yes — I've just read it again, too!)

> Enjoy your wishes and hopes for
> the new year — but take things
> quietly — God may have his own
> plans for you today.

10 JANUARY

Although we spend some time in the country and can see 'the real thing', nevertheless one of our delights each January is to notice when the snowdrops first appear on the barrows of the London flower sellers.

When Jan was a little girl I always used to bring her a bunch of snowdrops home as soon as I saw them. Her face would light up, she would put them in a special little jug she liked and she would look so happy, as if I'd brought her the most precious thing in the world. Well, I had, in a way, hadn't I? When she lived in America, I faithfully rang her up as soon as the snowdrops were on the barrows and told her that I had bought a bunch for her and put them in the little jug she liked so much.

Nature is but a name for an effect whose cause is God.

William Cowper (1731–1800)

10

After the war, when Scottie left the RAF, we bought our little mews house near Lancaster Gate, where we have lived ever since. I was working in the theatre in the West End of London by then, and in 1948 I was put under contract by J. Arthur Rank, whose film studies were at Denham.

Now, to get to the studios from Lancaster Gate very early in the morning was a four-part journey — and one of the hardest, most complicated I've ever had to make: a 'pre-dawn' walk to the Underground, then a tube train to the mainline station, then a train journey, then a 'workman's bus' to Denham, where the studios were. All of us 'bit-part' actors and extras used to watch with envy the 'stars' arriving in their chauffeur-driven cars, and dream . . .

The day came when I was given a bigger part, in a film starring Margaret Lockwood, and I felt I could afford a hire car to deliver me to and pick me up from the studios — ten pounds it cost. It was a bitterly cold winter, and after the first day's filming I thought, 'Oh bliss — I've a car coming to pick me up and whisk me home, in comfort!'

It was just beginning to snow, a few light flakes floating in the freezing dark, and as I got into the car I asked the driver to drive past the bus stop where I had previously caught a bus on the first part of my journey home each night. At the bus stop stood two old men and three old ladies, all extras, waiting for the bus. I wound down the window and called out, 'Anyone going to Lancaster Ga . . .?' Long before I could finish the sentence — tssss — they were all in the car with me, and I drove home sitting on an elderly man's knee — quite happy and comfortable!

> Don't curse the darkness — light a
> candle!
>
> *Chinese proverb*

12 JANUARY

So often we find ourselves visiting friends in hospital at this time of year, and it was one January that I had to go in for my own heart by-pass operation . . . It's a miracle, that operation.

There is no doubt that just after Christmas can be a low time for people, and often our health is affected. William Barclay wrote many prayers for people facing illness, and here's one for anyone who is facing a hospital visit at the moment.

> O God, my Father,
> Now that I know that I must go
> into hospital,

help me not to worry.
Help me to realize that worry only
makes things worse,
and that the more I worry the
longer I will take to get better.
Teach me that I am just as near you
in a hospital bed as in my own
home.
Give me that peace of mind
without which I know that I can't
have health of body.
Let me learn what Paul learned:
'I have learned, in whatever state I
am, to be content.'

William Barclay
Prayers for Help and Healing

13 JANUARY
—

You will probably have heard me say many
times by now that my mother was a living
wonder — with a heart that seemed to beat solely
for the purpose of helping people. Her door was
always open, and every day there would be at
least one 'Rat-tat' and a voice calling 'Are you
there, Mrs Hird? Can you lend us . . .' Whatever
it was — cup of vinegar, two candles, brown
paper and string — my mother was always ready
with a smile and a 'Yes, of course, love.' The rest
of us sometimes felt we should hang a big sign
up over the door saying 'We never Close!'

The Bellman perceived that their
spirits were low,
And repeated in musical tone
Some jokes he had kept for a
season of woe —
But the crew would do nothing but
groan.

Lewis Carroll (1832–98)
The Hunting of the Snark

14 JANUARY

No one knew more about comic timing than
my Dad. It's very difficult to tell anyone in
words how to do it. We talk about 'timing', but
I think it's easier to understand if you think of
it more as finding the *rhythm*, rather like music.
Every action, every sentence, every word even,
has a beat to it. Do it on one beat . . . nothing.
Choose another beat . . . tragedy. But get the
comic beat — and you raise the roof.

My Dad showed me how to get a laugh out
of the smallest bits of 'business', like hanging a
coat on a hook — just by breaking down the
simple action into its comic rhythm. Not even
the audience will really know *why* they are
laughing — but laugh they will!

Thank you, James Henry Hird — your good
teaching has given me a life in comedy.

15 JANUARY

— · —

Now Scottie doesn't look funny, and he's never been a comic, but 'my feller' makes me laugh more than anyone. It's little things, like the many times I've dropped one of my 'invisible' hair-nets on the bedroom floor, and Scottie will come in, to find me on my hand and knees patting the floor, and ask, 'Thor! What have you lost now?'

And I'll say, 'Can you see my See-No hair-net?'

I love the look on his face as he says, 'How do you expect me to "see" a See-No hair-net!?'

> When the people applauded him
> wildly, he turned to one of his
> friends and said, 'Have I said
> something foolish?'
>
> *Diogenes Laertius (c. 150 BC)*

16 JANUARY

— · —

When I put the wrong year on my cheques each new January, you know the way you do, I'm sometimes not just one year out, but two or three . . .

> Time, you old gipsy man,
> Will you not stay,

Put up your caravan
Just for one day?

Ralph Hodgson (1871–1962)
Poems (1917)

17 JANUARY
——

At this time of year the Hindus have a winter festival for Making Peace with Neighbours. Now that sounds like a great idea to me. We could all join in with that, couldn't we?

And it's also about now that Muslims celebrate the journey of Muhammad from Mecca to the Rock in Jerusalem, and then up to heaven, all in a single night. Scottie and I saw the Dome of the Rock Mosque in Jerusalem when we were there.

It's at this time of year that Christians hold a Week of Prayer for Christian Unity. Personally, I'm already very happy and united in any Christian church I find myself in. I was brought up a Methodist, have practically been 'adopted' by the Salvation Army, and regularly attend our little village Church of England church — a real ecu-maniac!

God has many names, though he is only one being.

Aristotle

Talking about the Church of England — how many of you ever read a column called 'Church News' in the 'posh' papers? To be honest, I don't read those sort of newspapers myself, but 'my attention is drawn . . .' as they say, to an item headed Clergy Appointments. And you'll have to believe me, this was hot from the press, the latest news from the Church of England (deep breath here, Thora):

> The Revd Jonathan Falkner, Priest-in-charge of Flixton; Homersfield; S. Elmham St Margaret; S. Elmham St Peter and S. Elmham St Cross; and also Rumburgh with S. Elmham All Saints; S. Elmham St James and S. Elmham St Michael with The Ilketshalls: to be Rector/Vicar, benefice of S. Elmham St Cross; S. Elmham St James; S. Elmham St Margaret; S. Elmham St Michael; S. Elmham St Peter; Rumburgh with S. Elmham All Saints; Flixton; Homersfield; Ilketshall St John; Ilketshall St Lawrence and Ilketshall St Margaret (St Emundsbury and Ipswich).

And good luck to you, Revd Jonathan Falkner! I hope you've got a sturdy bicycle for all the

Sunday services . . . And there's one thing I'm sure of — you're not going to have time to read this!

19 JANUARY

Our fireplace in Cheapside was a typical kitchen range of iron with an oven on the right-hand side. It was never used for roasting the meat or making the Yorkshire Pudding in my day, because there was a crack in it somewhere, but it served honourably as a receptacle for our pyjamas and bed slippers which were popped in there about an hour before bedtime. Oh those cold northern winters!

As kids, we undressed in front of the fire, opened the oven door, pyjamas out — quick, and there you were, in hot pyjamas, hot bedroom slippers, drinking even hotter cocoa! All as a preliminary to going upstairs to our frozen bedrooms. We rushed upstairs into bed, and moved the stone hot water bottles, which Mother had placed just where our little bottoms would nestle, down to the bottom of the bed to warm our feet. Bedrooms were always cold in those days, weren't they? It was long before anyone had central heating.

> And nobody knows
> (Tiddely pom),
> How cold my toes

18

(Tiddely pom),
How cold my toes
(Tiddely pom),
Are growing.

A.A. Milne (1882–1956)
House at Pooh Corner (1928)

20 JANUARY

On freezing nights, when my brother Neville was older and came home from work for his tea, to wash and change to go out, he'd always put his pyjamas on *under* his suit, so that when he came home again he only had to take off his outer garments — and presto! he was all ready for bed!

I was reminded of Nev doing that recently, when I was in Canterbury Cathedral for evensong one night, and I noticed that the lady next to me was wearing her nightie, dressing gown and slippers under her overcoat! Very sensible!

Sunshine let it be or frost,
Storm or calm, as thou shalt
   choose;
Though thine every gift were lost,
Thee thyself we could not lose.

Mary E. Coleridge (1861–1907)

21 JANUARY

Always the first flower in our garden to welcome the new year is the little aconite . . .

Earth has borne a little son:
He is a very little one:
He has a head of golden hair
And a grave unwinking stare.
He wears a bib all frilled and green
Round his neck to keep him clean,
Though before another spring
A thousand children Earth may
   bring
Forth to bud and blossoming —
Lily daughters — cool and slender,
Roses passionate and tender,
Tulip sons as brave as swords,
Hollyhocks like laughing lords —
Yet she'll never love them quite
As much as she loves aconite —
Aconite — the first of all,
Who is so very, very small,
Who is so golden-haired and good,
And wears a bib as babies should.

A.M. Graham
The Golden Staircase (1928)

20

22 JANUARY

— —

Have you ever heard of the ancient Japanese verse form, the 'haiku'? I hadn't myself until recently, when I was listening to a programme about them on the radio. The Japanese have been writing them for hundreds of years, and it's as popular with them as the limerick is here.

Now pay attention, while I get a bit technical. Only, if you understand the rules, you'll get more out of reading the haiku. A haiku is a three-line poem, with exactly seventeen syllables: the first and third lines must have five syllables, the second line has seven. They are about the seasons, and the mysteries of nature, and a good haiku will usually contain a paradox or a surprise.

> No oil to read by
> I am off to bed but ah!
> My moonlit pillow.
> *Basho (1644–94)*
> *trans. Peter Beilenson*

23 JANUARY

— —

Is it just me, or have you also noticed how more and more people seem to talk about Chinese horoscopes and the Chinese New Year — which begins at this time?

Each Chinese year is named after one of the

twelve symbols — either a bird or an animal — of the Chinese Zodiac, and it's meant to be extremely lucky for you whenever it's the year of the animal or bird you were born under. Which should mean that each of us is lucky every twelve years.

Unfortunately, as I don't know what my sign *is*, I don't know which year to look out for — but other people seem to. 'Oh, yes, I'm a Pig!' they say — or a Rat or a Cat or a Rooster . . .. Come to think of it — I'm not sure that I really *do* want to know what I am!

> For he is our God; and we are the
> people of his pasture, and the sheep
> of his hand.
>
> *Psalm 95:7*

24 JANUARY

I know I'm not an angel, but my mother was an angel, and my daughter is an angel, and the Lord knows — because I tell him every day — that I have been so thankful for both of them all my life.

> Faithfulness in little things is a big
> thing.
>
> *St John Chrysostom*

25 JANUARY

— —

It's a wee while now since Scottie and I took the high road to Forfar, where his father's family all hailed from, but we'll still raise a glass each Burns Night — for auld lang syne . . .

> Some hae meat and canna eat,
> And some would eat that want it;
> But we hae meat, and we can eat,
> And sae the Lord be thank it.
>
> Robert Burns (1759–96)
> The Selkirk Grace

26 JANUARY

— —

At this time of year The Variety Club — you know, the Barkers — have a big drive to raise money for charity, and they give awards to people in the world of entertainment. You could say that Scottie and I both grew up in that world. I know the lives of entertainers sometimes seem very peculiar to people not in 'the business', as we call it. Some very talented people go through the whole of their professional lives without ever 'making it' to the top, scarcely earning enough to live on. At the other extreme are those — often very young men and women — who are paid vast sums of money, and perhaps not every member of the public thinks they quite deserve it!

But I don't think I know of a single entertainer — young or old — who has done well out of our business, who hasn't been well aware of how fortunate they are, and been more than willing to 'give back' — by giving their time and famous name to help raise money for charitable causes.

> Ye are the light of the world. A city that is set on an hill cannot be hid. Neither do men light a candle, and put it under a bushel, but on a candlestick; and it giveth light unto all that are in the house. Let your light so shine before men, that they may see your good works, and glorify your Father which is in heaven. *Matthew 5:14–16*

27 JANUARY

As the month draws to its end you can almost 'feel' the days stretching as the evenings close in a little later each day. I always start to feel much more cheerful — I've never liked the cold and dark — and it's so lovely when you can look out of the window after a cup of afternoon tea, and still see daylight.

> Christ has turned all our sunsets into dawns.
> *St Clement of Alexandria*

The Darkling Thrush

I leant upon a coppice gate
When frost was spectre-gray,
And winter's dregs made desolate
The weakening eye of day.
The tangled bine-stems scored the sky
Like strings of broken lyres,
And all mankind that haunted night
Had sought their household fires . . .

At once a voice arose among
The bleak twigs overhead
In a full-hearted evensong
Of joy illimited;
An aged thrush, frail, gaunt, and small,
In blast-beruffled plume,
Had chosen thus to fling his soul
Upon the growing gloom.

So little cause for carollings
Of such ecstatic sound
Was written on terrestrial things
Afar or nigh around,
That I could think there trembled through
His happy good-night air
Some blessed hope, whereof he knew
And I was unaware.

Thomas Hardy (1840–1928)

29 JANUARY

——

That lovely poem by Thomas Hardy has reminded me about a blackbird that used to regularly visit our bird table.

We've always fed the birds in winter, and years ago one of my best friends from school, Mabel Bagshaw, told me what her old father had told her, just before he died, when she was looking after him and thinking how much she was going to miss him. He had said that he'd come back and visit her . . . as a blackbird!

On one of my visits to Morecambe I was having tea with Mabel and I saw a lovely blackbird in her garden. I remarked about it to her and she said, 'Oh yes, it's me dad!'

> He is not to be gotten or holden by
>   thought,
> only by love.
>   *Julian of Norwich (c.1342–after 1413)*

30 JANUARY

——

Septuagesima

Seventy days until Easter — it's not long between Christmas and Easter, is it?

I wonder as I wander, out under the
sky,
How Jesus the Saviour did come for to
die
For poor orn'ry people like you and like
I . . .
I wonder as I wander, out under the
sky.

When Mary bore Jesus, 'twas in a cow's
stall,
With wise men and animals and
shepherds and all.
But high from the heavens a star's light
did fall,
And the promise of ages it then did
recall.

If Jesus had wanted for any wee thing,
A star in the sky or a bird on the wing,
Or all of God's angels in heaven for to
sing,
He could surely have had it, 'cause he
was the King.

I wonder as I wander, out under the
sky,
How Jesus the Saviour did come for to
die
For poor orn'ry people like you and like
I . . .
I wonder as I wander, out under the sky.
North Carolina hymn – traditional

31 JANUARY

—·—

On the last Sunday of the month, my first 'trail' for my series *Praise Be!* is shown on television at the end of *Songs of Praise*. There I'll be in my best hat — perhaps with a newborn lamb in my arms! — to ask viewers to send me their requests for their favourite hymns.

Like the lighter evenings, and the birds singing in the mornings, and the flowers in the garden, the loving letters that start arriving now are beautiful harbingers of spring!

> Praise the Lord! Praise the Lord!
> Let the people rejoice!

FEBRUARY

Arise! shine; for thy light is come,
and the glory of the Lord is risen
upon thee.

Isaiah 60:1

1 FEBRUARY

- -

The one thing you can never be sure of, in these beautiful British Isles of ours, is exactly what the weather is going to do next. But the one month you can be *almost* sure will be very cold is February. December and January can surprise you by being mild and almost 'spring-like', but February — brrrrrr!

> As the days lengthen, the cold strengthens.
>
> *Old weather proverb*

2 FEBRUARY

- -

It may be cold outside, but indoors February is a month of lights and music. At Candlemas Christians celebrate, traditionally with long candle-lit processions, the Presentation of Jesus in the Temple.

The millions of little candles lit today in churches all over the world still tell the same story of how Jesus is the 'light to lighten the Gentiles' — because St Luke says that when Mary offered her baby son to the Lord, in the Temple in Jerusalem, an old man called Simeon, who had been waiting all his life for God's Messiah to come, took Jesus in his arms, blessed God and said:

Lord, now lettest thou thy servant
depart in peace, according to thy
word:
For mine eyes have seen thy
salvation,
Which thou hast prepared before
the face of all people;
A light to lighten the Gentiles, and
the glory of thy people Israel.

Luke 2:29–32

3 FEBRUARY

——

I won't pretend that I understand all the poetry
of the late T.S. Eliot, because I don't . . . But
sometimes he wrote lines so simple and
beautiful, that when I read them I think, 'You
clever man. I wish I'd written that!'

We thank thee for the lights that
    we have kindled,
The light of altar and sanctuary;
Small lights of those who meditate
    at midnight
And lights directed through the
    coloured panes of windows
And light reflected from the
    polished stone,
The gilded carven wood, the
    coloured fresco.
Our gaze is submarine, our eyes

look upward
And see the light that fractures
   through unquiet water.
We see the light but see not whence
   it comes.
O Light Invisible, we glorify thee!

In our rhythm of earthly life we
   tire of light. We are glad when
the day ends, when the play ends;
   and ecstasy is too much
      pain.
We are children quickly tired:
children who are up in the night
   and
fall asleep as the rocket is fired;
   and the day is long for
      work or play . . .

T.S. Eliot (1888–1965)
The Rock (1934)

4 FEBRUARY

I wonder if anyone remembers the Edwardian
movement for 'Pleasant Sunday Afternoons' . . .
do you? In Victorian days, apart from going to
church, 'respectable' people stayed at home and
read 'improving books' or the Holy Bible on
'the Sabbath'. There were no entertainments and
they would have been shocked to see anyone
doing anything so frivolous as reading a novel!

I loved my Sunday School and I know from my *Praise Be!* letters that many children of my generation went both morning and afternoon, sometimes walking a mile or two there and back each time, so the whole of Sunday was completely taken up with religion.

But the movement for 'Pleasant Sunday Afternoons' must have reached Morecambe, because I also have very happy memories of the Sunday concerts in our pavilion on the end of Central Pier. These concerts were different from the regular weekday concert parties — with their excellent artistes 'The Superbs', 'Frills and Flounces', 'The Pelicans', to name but a few . . . The Sunday concerts gave us our 'bit of culture': Herr Von Beck, the famous cellist, and his orchestra . . . And very nice it was too!

> Next to theology I give to music
> the highest place and honour.
> Music is the art of the prophets, the
> only art that can calm the agitations
> of the soul; it is one of the most
> magnificent and delightful presents
> God has given us.
> *Martin Luther (1483–1546)*

5 FEBRUARY

Did you notice in that last bit how I called it *'our'* pavilion? There is no doubt that the

Central Pier and its pavilion was not just part of our life during the time that my father was Manager there — it *was* our life. Oh! the long and happy hours Nev and I and all our friends spent on that pier! The antics we got up to, the excitement, the jobs we had — all these things were handed to us on a plate during the period in which we grew up from very small children to teenagers.

> Thou hast given so much to me . . .
> Give one thing more — a grateful heart.
>
> *George Herbert (1593–1633)*

6 FEBRUARY

One of the features of the Central Pier Pavilion that I admired greatly as a child was the iron sheet or safety curtain. It was lovely! John Birkett, a Morecambe chemist, distilled his own perfume, and hired the entire safety curtain to advertise 'AMO—DEL'.

The picture on the curtain was of an Indian canoe full of flowers floating down a wide river with an Indian, complete with feathers, paddling along in his canoe. The background was mountains in hazy mauves and blues, and the lettering read 'AMO—DEL — The Gathered Fragrance of Indian Dales'.

I thought it was beautiful!

By the shores of Gitche Gumee,
By the shining Big-Sea-Water,
Stood the wigwam of Nokomis,
Daughter of the Moon, Nokomis.
Dark behind it rose the forest,
Rose the black and gloomy pine-trees,
Rose the firs with cones upon them;
Bright before it beat the water,
Beat the clear and sunny water,
Beat the shining Big-Sea-Water.

Henry Longfellow (1807–82)
Hiawatha

7 FEBRUARY

I suppose I've been going on rather a lot about the Central Pier, and my childhood days. To tell you the truth, in February that's just what Scottie and I spend a lot of our time doing — reminiscing. It's too cold to go out — I don't like the cold — so apart from doing the books, answering letters, and rehearsing and recording any acting jobs I may have, any spare time is spent sitting by the fire having a good old natter.

I realize how lucky we are, both in our eighties, to still have each other to chat to, with so many shared memories to talk over, and still enjoying each other's company — I can honestly say there's never a dull moment.

We shall not cease from exploration
And the end of all our exploring
Will be to arrive where we started
And know the place for the first time.
                              T.S. Eliot
                    Little Gidding (1942)

8 FEBRUARY

Scottie and I are like the couple in this Victorian
poem. The Victorian poets wrote the 'pop'
songs of their day!

Fast falls the snow, O lady mine,
Sprinkling the lawn with crystals fine,
But by the gods we won't repine
While we're together,
We'll chat and rhyme and kiss and
    dine,
Defying weather.

So stir the fire and pour the wine,
And let those sea-green eyes divine
Pour their love-madness into mine:
I don't care whether
'Tis snow or sun or rain or shine
If we're together.
                    Mortimer Collins (1876)

—•—

Everyone is asked to send their *Praise Be!* letters
to the BBC, so the Religious Department
receive them first, but quite a few seem to find
their way directly to me. I have to send them
on to the *Praise Be!* office — so the hymn
requests can be sorted out — but I love reading
them as they come in.

People are so kind and say such loving things
to welcome me back 'into their living rooms'
as so many of them put it. You cannot know
what pleasure they give me. I show them to
Scottie, and as often as not there'll be a mention
of him and Jan somewhere in the letter, too.
And so many of them end, 'Give my love to
Scottie and your lovely daughter, Jan.' Oh, it's
just like a big, happy family reunion!

> Happy are they, they that love God,
> Whose hearts have Christ confest,
> Who by his cross have found their life,
> And 'neath his yoke their rest.
>
> Glad is the praise, sweet are the songs,
> When they together sing;
> And strong the prayers that bow the
>   ear
> Of heaven's eternal King.
>   *Yattenden Hymnal*

10 FEBRUARY

I know the *Praise Be!* production team try to be
very fair, and the hymns are selected on the
basis of the number of requests we receive for
each one. But I confess that sometimes I come
across a letter from someone to whom it would
make such a big difference to have their hymn
included, and then I do try to influence things!
Some of the letters move me to tears — literally.
Unfortunately I can never manage to give a
mention to all the names of all the people I
would like to include — if only the programmes
could be three hours long, instead of thirty-five
minutes!

> Can I see another's woe,
> And not be in sorrow too?
> Can I see another's grief,
> And not seek for kind relief?
> *William Blake (1757–1827)*
> *On Another's Sorrow*

11 FEBRUARY

Every year — with only one exception, which
I'll tell you about later — by far the most letters
ask for one particular hymn, as anyone who
regularly watches *Praise Be!* will know — 'The
Old Rugged Cross'. Don't you love hearing a
Salvation Army band play that tune when

they're out and about our city streets?

> On a hill far away stood an old rugged
> cross
> The emblem of suffering and shame;
> And I love that old cross, where the
> dearest and best
> For a world of lost sinners was slain.
> So I'll cherish the old rugged cross
> 'Til my trophies at last I lay down;
> I will cling to the old rugged cross
> And exchange it some day for a
> crown.
> *The Revd George Bennard (1913)*

12 FEBRUARY

Here's another prayer from that wise Scotsman,
Dr William Barclay's book *The Plain Man's Book
of Prayers*. I don't know about you, but I
sometimes find the dark days of February quite
a trial to get through.

> O God, our Father, help us through
> this day to live that we may bring help
> to others, credit to ourselves and the
> name we bear, and joy to those who
> love us, and to thee.
>
> Help us to be:
>   Cheerful when things go wrong;

Persevering when things are
difficult;
Serene when things are irritating.

Enable us to be:
Helpful to those in difficulties;
Kind to those in need;
Sympathetic to those whose
hearts are sore and sad.

Grant that:
Nothing may make us lose our
temper;
Nothing may take away our joy;
Nothing may ruffle our peace;
Nothing may make us bitter
towards any man.

So grant that all through this day
all with whom we work, and all
whom we meet, may see in us the
reflection of the Master, whose we
are, and whom we seek to serve.
This we ask for thy love's sake.
Amen.

William Barclay

13 FEBRUARY

I love the sound when schoolchildren are let out
of their classrooms in 'break' and come out into
the playground for ten minutes. The scene is

41

still almost exactly the same as it was when I was at school — one group competing with a skipping rope; two little girls going round, heads together, telling 'secrets'; other children chasing and playing 'tag' with much screaming and laughter. The only difference is that today you'll see quite a few on their own, absorbed in some 'Sonic the Hedgehog' thing.

I was on a radio programme a little while ago, called *The Tingle Factor*, and one of the sounds I chose that gave me 'a tingle' was the one made by children in a school playground during break!

> I heard the glorious song coming
>   out of heaven,
> The sweetest music ever heard;
> I heard a mighty song sung by all
>   the angels,
> My soul thrilled at every loving
>   word.
>   *'I heard a thousand trumpets'*

14 FEBRUARY
- -
St Valentine's Day

When I've time, I like to make my own old-fashioned Valentine cards out of coloured lace, which you can still find on market stalls in the North of England. Then I write my own little rhymes to go inside. I make 'em for Scottie and the family, kindly note — not some 'leading man!' (Well, Scottie *is* my 'leading man'!)

> Yet mark'd I where the bolt of
>   Cupid fell:
> It fell upon a little western flower,
> Before milk-white, now purple
>   with love's wound,
> And maidens call it, Love-in-
>   idleness.
>> *William Shakespeare (1564–1616)*
>> *A Midsummer–Night's Dream*

15 FEBRUARY

In spite of the cold, some of last year's pansies — the 'love-in-idleness' Puck was describing in that last bit — are still in flower in the cottage garden. God bless 'em.

There are bits of colour all over the garden now, with snowdrops, aconites and crocuses; trees coming more and more into bud; and the daffodil shoots slowly forming their flower buds, so there will be a mass of yellow in a week or two. It never fails to fill me with wonder, even after seeing it happen every spring for eighty years now!

> You will find something far greater
> in the woods than you will in

books. Stones and trees will teach
you what you can never learn from
masters.

St Bernard of Clairvaux

16 FEBRUARY

I haven't seen any wild geese lately. I wonder
if they've left us for another year. Here's
another of those haikus I was talking about —
I heard it on the radio, and it's rather how I feel.

> I know the wild geese
> Will come and eat the barley
> But oh! When they go . . .

17 FEBRUARY

The prize-winning example of my wonderful
mother's generosity was when a tearful young
woman came to the door one Sunday
lunchtime. Amid sobs she informed my mother
that her young husband's father and mother
had turned up unexpectedly. (Anyone who lives
at the seaside will know from their own
experience that you are expected to run a free
boarding house for relatives who suddenly
fancy a breath of sea air!)

She said, 'I — er — feel awful asking you this,
Mrs Hird — but have you done a roast? Er —

I'll bring it back after.' Now just stop there for a minute . . . Right. You do realize what she was asking, don't you? She was asking my mother to hand over our family lunch!

I can still remember my dad's expression as he very carefully and deliberately folded the *Sunday Chronicle* and put it down while he awaited developments. Almost in an instant my mother had produced a large black japanned tray, and onto it went the still-sizzling joint of sirloin beef that she had just been about to carve.

'You'd better take the vegetables as well,' my mother was saying. The next item was the gravy, then a large apple pie and a glass jug of custard waltzed their way on to the tray, as my mother was advising, 'You'd better go out the back way, love, then nobody will see you!'

After a few moments my mother, who was still in the back kitchen, started — very softly — to sing a few bars of 'Oh where is my boy tonight?' And then, just as though it was the normal routine to go to all that trouble to cook a big dinner for your loved ones and then give it all away, she called out, 'Can you eat two fried eggs with your bacon, Jim love?'

By now my father was viewing the table, the white linen cloth, Victorian silver cruet, linen serviettes in our individual rings. 'Yes please,' replied James Henry, in the voice he used when playing kings or Roman emperors — still contemplating the table. 'That will be very nice

45

with horseradish sauce!' (Mother had forgotten
to add that to the overladen tray!!)

> What wee gave, wee have;
> What wee spent, wee had;
> What wee kept, wee lost.
>> *Epitaph on Edward Courtenay*
>> *Earl of Devonshire (d.1419)*

18 FEBRUARY

Scottie's dad was Musical Director at various
theatres, and taught the 'cello, and played it very
well himself, while my dad moved along in the
entertainment business from artist to Manager,
and was hot-stuff on the banjo! It was a great
moment when we discovered that 'the two
Jameses' (my dad and Scottie's dad were both
called James) had both at one time been
Managers for Charles Poole, the pioneer of the
Panorama, Cyclorama and Mirrorama.

They were forms of illusion. Scenes were
projected from a magic lantern onto a revolving
canvas. For instance, 'The Siege of Mafeking'
was produced quite realistically by adding gun
noises, flashes and a background of smoke,
while cut out figures of carriages and horses
fixed to a guaze would move one way, and
clouds went in the opposite direction. My
father even appeared in a Cyclorama film in
those early days. He rode up into the clouds on

a bicycle! This magical effect was achieved by laying a sky-and-cloud painted backcloth on the ground and riding across it normally and then turning the backcloth on its side. Get it? Clever stuff, eh?

They were really the forerunners of the film industry. Very 'ahead', our two dads!

> Art is much less important than life
> — but what a poor life without it.
> *Robert Motherwell*

19 FEBRUARY

Even in 1905 people were thinking up excuses for not going to church . . .

Reasons for Not Going to Church: No. 1
The young woman in the front of the queue for Gallery 5 means to stay away from church till the weather is milder, because she has had a nasty cold since last Wednesday. No, it was not while standing in the rain for twenty-five minutes on Tuesday night, when she went to the Panorama, that she got it. It was in church on the Sabbath before. Two people were late, and each time the door opened

she felt a rush of cold air on her
left shoulder, and she knew she was
'in for it'.
The Morning Watch, February 1905

20 FEBRUARY
— —

Scottie and I are both a pair of early birds, never
up later than 6.30 in the mornings — and
sometimes much earlier than that. For many
years it was a case of having to. I still find it's
a good time for learning words, before the
telephone starts ringing, and even when I don't
have to get up for any reason, I always wake up
early. I've never been one to stay in bed once
I'm awake — I don't suppose I'll change now.

I sometimes think early-morning Breakfast
Television was invented especially for us!

Awake, awake: fling off the night!
for God has sent his glorious light;
And we who live in Christ's new day
must works of darkness put away.

Then sing for joy, and use each day;
give thanks for everything alway
Lift up your hearts; with one accord
praise God through Jesus Christ our
Lord.

J.R. Peacey (b. 1896)

21 FEBRUARY

— —

Scottie and I both enjoy watching television when we get the chance. I know people who say, 'Oh, we hardly ever watch television.' I think, well, you don't know what you're missing!

We enjoy watching the afternoon quizzes — it helps to keep our brains active! — and the children's programmes are excellent. I like nothing better than when I'm asked to read one of the stories for *Jackanory*, or to take part in a good children's television drama, like *Goggle-eyes*.

> Between the dark and the daylight
> When the night is beginning to
> lower,
> Comes a pause in the day's
> occupations,
> That is known as the Children's
> Hour.
>
> *Henry Longfellow (1807–82)*

22 FEBRUARY

— —

Talking of Children's Hour — I sometimes wonder what goes on in school lessons today. I mean, I like to think of myself as a reasonably helpful person — but however was I to answer this?

Dear Thora,
We're doing 'God' next term. Please
supply us with full details.
Yours sincerely,
All in Lower Third

23 FEBRUARY

The Royalty Theatre and Opera House,
Morecambe:
'A compact, comfortable and well-appointed
place of entertainment, lavishly decorated
throughout and one of the most comfortable
outside of London, a handsome stone structure,
in the classic style. Designed by Frank
Matcham. First opened 4 April 1898.'
But when the bulldozers left and the dust
finally settled on the morning of Monday 23
February 1970, it had been completely
demolished — in the name of progress . . .
Neville, my brother, and Scottie and I visited
the site later that year, to pay our last respects,
and we stood there for ages, just looking and
remembering, although all that there was left to
see were stones and grey dust.

The tumult and the shouting dies;
The captains and the kings depart:
Still stands thine ancient sacrifice,
An humble and a contrite heart.
Lord God of Hosts, be with us yet,

> Lest we forget — lest we forget.
> *Rudyard Kipling (1865–1936)*
> *Recessional (1897)*

24 FEBRUARY

There are some jobs that need to be done in the garden in February. Weeds start appearing at the slightest suggestion of rain or warmth — however short-lived. And on the lines of 'a stitch in time saves nine' any piece of couch grass uprooted now will save hours of back-breaking digging once it really gets going later in the year. Some of the autumn flowering clematis have to be cut right back, so if you're a novice gardener or have moved to a new part of the country, keep looking over the fence at what your neighbour's doing, and do the same!

> Few are born to do the great work
> of the world, but the work that all
> can do is to make a small home
> circle brighter and better.
> *George Eliot (1819–80)*

25 FEBRUARY

However many jobs you *ought* to be doing in the garden — it's not much good trying to do them when everything has disappeared under a few inches of snow! But how lovely to go out in the garden on a sunny morning, and see the snowdrops still looking so fresh and green — flowering bravely through a snowdrift!

> One month is past, another is begun,
> Since merry bells rang out the
>   dying year,
> And buds of rarest green began to
>   peer,
> As if impatient for a warmer sun;
> And tho' the distant hills are bleak
>   and dun,
> The virgin snowdrop, like a
>   lambent fire,
> Pierces the cold earth with its
>   green-streaked spire
> And in dark woods, the wandering
>   little one,
> May find a primrose.
>   *Hartley Coleridge (1796–1849)*

26 FEBRUARY

Sometimes on a particularly dark February day, Jan will come round to the cottage door and invite us over for what she calls 'a taste of summer'. I feel quite excited! I know she's going to take some home-grown raspberries out of the deep-freeze — and what a treat it always seems!

Let others tell of storms and
    showers,
I only count your sunny hours.
                    Engraved on a sundial

27 FEBRUARY

Scottie and I like to get away for a short break
somewhere warm in February. In recent years
we've been on some wonderful winter cruises
organized by SAGA. They are especially
arranged for retired people, and if you're old
enough to have retired but are still full of beans,
I can't speak too highly of them. Sometimes Jan
and William come on the cruise, too, and they
love it — so it isn't just old codgers like us who
go on them!

And oh, I do love a sea voyage! When we land
anywhere I say to the others, 'Go on! You go
off. I want to get on with my writing.'

Jan will say, 'No, Mummy, we can't leave you
on your own. Someone must stay with you.'

But I won't hear of it! I find myself a quiet
corner of the deck and settle down to a pleasant
couple of hours of looking out to sea, and
remembering, and writing down all the lovely
things that have happened . . .

O Lord, you have made us very
small, and we bring our years to an
end, like a tale that is told; help us

to remember that beyond our brief
day is the eternity of your love.
Reinhold Niebuhr (1893–1971)

28 FEBRUARY

Here's a prayer for anyone who is going away
on a journey, to bless you on your way.

> May the road rise to meet you,
> May the wind be always at your
> back,
> May the sun shine warm upon your
> face,
> The rains fall soft upon your fields
> and,
> Until we meet again,
> May God hold you in the palm of
> his hand.
> *Traditional Irish blessing*

54

MARCH

Prayer for St David
. . . He brought the church into
    our homes,
put the holy vessels on the
kitchen table
with bread from the pantry and
    wine from the cellar,
and he stood behind the table
like a tramp
so as not to hide from us the
    wonder of the sacrifice.
And after the Communion we had
    a talk round the fire
and he spoke to us of God's
natural order,
the person, the family, the nation
    and the society of
nations, and the cross, which
    prevents us from making any one
    of them into a god . . ..

1 MARCH

St David's Day, Patron Saint of Wales

Songs of Praise nearly always comes from a Welsh church or chapel on the first Sunday of March, and the congregation are all seen wearing daffodils in their button-holes. However late spring may be, there always seem to be enough daffodils in Wales for St Dafydd's Day. I wonder if that's why they call them 'daffodils' — you know, like Dafyd-dils?

St David died around the year 600, and they say his relics still lie in the shrine in St David's Cathedral.

> The world will never starve for
> want of wonders; but only for want
> of wonder.
> *G.K. Chesterton (1874–1936)*

2 MARCH

I remember one year on *Praise Be!* when, as usual, I had a great number of requests for the Welsh hymn 'Guide me, O thou great Redeemer' — and an equally large number of requests for 'Guide me, O thou great Jehovah'! So I read out all the requests alternately: Redeemer, *Jehovah,* Redeemer, *Jehovah* . . . as though all the viewers were having an argument — which clever Thora was then able to settle by showing an interview with the Prince of Wales — because he should know! He appeared on *Songs of Praise* that year and requested:

> Guide me, O thou great Redeemer,
> Pilgrim through this barren land;
> I am weak, but thou art mighty,
> Hold me with thy powerful hand:
> Bread of heaven
> Feed me till I want no more.
>
> *W. Williams (1717–91)*

P.S. In a way, everyone's right. The hymn was originally 'Guide me, O thou great Jehovah', inspired by the Old Testament story of the Exodus, and the Israelites' forty-year-long journey through the wilderness to the Promised Land. But some church hymn books changed it to 'Redeemer', because otherwise there would be no mention of Jesus.

3 MARCH
Ash Wednesday

> Remember, O man, dust thou art,
> and to dust thou shalt return.

At one Ash Wednesday service I went to, in a

London church, everyone was given a piece of paper and a pencil, as well as our hymn book and prayer book at the door. The vicar explained that he wanted us to write down everything we could think of that we had ever done wrong. A lot of chewing of pencils took place, and then all the bits of paper were collected and taken up to the altar.

We felt a bit anxious, you know, in case he was going to read them out! I could imagine everyone craning their necks round to see whose paper he was reading, like we did in class at school . . . But instead they were all burned in a little brazier. Then we all went up to the altar rail and knelt down, and he dipped his thumb in the ash from the burnt bits of paper, and smudged a little ashy cross on our foreheads. This was a sign that all the sins that we had written on our little bits of paper were forgiven.

> And the thief said unto Jesus,
> 'Lord, remember me when thou
> comest into thy kingdom.'
> And Jesus said unto him, 'Verily I
> say unto thee,
> Today shalt thou be with me in
> paradise.'
>
> *Luke 23:42–43*

4 MARCH

Once Lent begins — on Ash Wednesday — Catholic churches are stripped bare inside: no cloths or candles on the altars, no flowers on the pedestals. Not all Protestant and Non-Conformist churches do this. Yet in churches taking part in *Songs of Praise* on television, Protestant or Catholic, I notice that the vicar is *always* overruled by the Flower Arranging Committee!

In many churches the beautiful Ash Wednesday Prayer Book collect is said every Sunday during Lent.

Almighty and everlasting God
who hatest nothing that thou hast
    made,
and dost forgive the sins of all
    them that are penitent:
Create and make in us
new and contrite hearts,
that we, worthily lamenting our
    sins,
and acknowledging our
    wretchedness,
may obtain of thee, the God of all
    mercy,
perfect remission and forgiveness.
Amen.

Book of Common Prayer

5 MARCH

—-—

When the March winds do blow, we shall
  have snow,
and what will the robin do then, poor thing?

I love the old weather sayings, don't you? And
in my opinion, they are more likely to be
accurate than some of the scare stories we read
in the papers.

Even as a child I remember newspapers
frightening us with stories about 'what the
scientists say' about the weather. Whenever
there was a long, hot summer (which, let's face
it, wasn't very often) it wasn't enough just to
enjoy it. We had to be told, 'The earth is moving
nearer the sun and will explode.' But if the
summer was a particularly cold, wet one, they
said, 'The earth is moving *away* from the sun,
and there will be a second Ice Age.' I never knew
which prospect I liked least!

Nowadays it's 'holes in the ozone layer', and
after three hot summers they've been going on
about 'the greenhouse effect'. However, after
several months of cold and rain they've gone
strangely quiet about the greenhouse effect
recently . . . But before long, mark my words,
they will have thought up something else to
scare us with.

Phooey! Well, that's what I think.

> O ye hypocrites, ye can discern the
> face of the sky;
> but can ye not discern the signs of
> the times?
>
> *Matthew 16:3*

6 MARCH

A 'sight for sore eyes' in the countryside at this time of year, if you're lucky enough, are the 'mad' March hares, tearing through the frosty fields, and engaging in boxing matches. They sit perfectly still among twigs and leaves for hours, playing statues, and it's almost impossible to discover them. But when there's a sprinkling of snow on the ground, you may see one suddenly start to race about, followed by others. They seem enormous against the white snow, and you wonder how it was you couldn't see them before.

> O world invisible, we view thee,
> O world intangible, we touch thee,
> O world unknowable, we know
>   thee,
> Inapprehensible, we clutch thee!
> *Francis Thompson (1859–1907)*

7 MARCH

The word Lent comes from the word 'lengthen', and means that the days are getting longer and longer. Sometimes — 'when the March winds *do* blow' — it's tempting to wish they would pass a little more quickly, so that it could soon be April. But, as my mother told me, and I told Jan, and Jan told her children, and they will undoubtedly tell their children . . . you mustn't start wishing your life away!

> As if you could kill time without injuring eternity.
> *Henry David Thoreau (1817–62)*

8 MARCH

Holi

We could do worse than to brighten ourselves up at this time of year by joining in the high-spirited Hindu spring festival of Holi that falls today. They have bonfires, singing, processions and dances; and coloured powder and water is scattered and squirted over everybody. Can you imagine seeing those upright, respectable, dark-suited, bowler-hatted gentlemen in the City, being splashed all over with bright colours? Well, it wouldn't do them any harm, I reckon.

O God,
Let us be united;
Let us speak in harmony;
Let our minds apprehend alike.
Common be our prayer;
Common be the end of our
assembly;
Common be our resolution;
Common be our deliberations.
Alike be our feelings;
Unified be our hearts;
Common be our intentions;
Perfect be our unity.

Hindu Scriptures (Rig-Veda)

9 MARCH

Sometimes on *Praise Be!* I'd be filmed in March visiting places where our old favourite hymns were written, like the rock at Burrington Combe, in the Mendip Hills in Somerset. It was beautiful, but bitterly cold, the day I went.

It may only be a legend, but it's said that Augustus Toplady thought of the words for his wonderful hymn, 'Rock of Ages', while sheltering from a thunderstorm in a cleft in a rock. He didn't actually write the hymn there and then — in fact it was not until long after he had left his parish in the Mendips. But who says the memory of that day sheltering in the rock didn't come back to inspire him years later? Any road up, the words are beautiful, whatever inspired them!

> Nothing in my hand I bring,
> Simply to thy cross I cling.
>> *A.M. Toplady (1740–78)*

10 MARCH

Another place I had the pleasure of visiting for *Praise Be!* was Horbury Bridge, near Wakefield in Yorkshire. It was there that in 1864 Sabine Baring-Gould, who was curate-in-charge of the mission church, sat up all one Whit Sunday night to write a hymn suitable for his Sunday School children to sing the next morning as they marched along in procession to a neighbouring village for a united Whit Monday festival. The hymn? 'Onward Christian Soldiers' of course — my own favourite!

> Onward, then, ye people,
> Join our happy throng,
> Blend with ours your voices
> In the triumph song:
> Glory, laud, and honour
> Unto Christ the King,
> This through countless ages
> Men and angels sing.
> Onward, Christian soldiers,
> Marching as to war,

With the cross of Jesus
Going on before!
Revd S. Baring-Gould (1834–1924)

11 MARCH
— —

It's been mild enough to take little walks down
the lane in Sussex recently — providing we
wrap up well. The hedgerows are still rather
bare, except for the white blackthorn flowers,
which appear before the leaves. But there are
hundreds of daffodils about now, and we might
find some pink-purple wood-anemones . . .

Have you noticed how funny the little
chaffinches are, when you go down country
lanes? I sometimes think they are coming along
the road with us, keeping us company, flying
from bush to bush, singing 'Tsip . . . cheeer .
. . tsip . . . cheeer!'

> Are not two sparrows sold for a
> farthing? and one of them shall not
> fall to the ground without your
> Father. But the very hairs of your
> head are all numbered.
> Fear ye not therefore, ye are of
> more value than many sparrows.
> *Matthew 10:29–31*

12 MARCH
— —

Haiku for March
Yesterday — sunshine,
Today — I'm freezing! Quick,
March!
Please make up your mind!

All my own work! Have you tried one yet?

13 MARCH
— —

Mothering Sunday

In the old days, everyone would go home for
Mothering Sunday — to their Mother church.
We have a special family service in our own
little church, and Jan and I both love to go. The
Sunday School children bring little pots of
primroses to give to their mothers. Then they
give primroses to all the mothers whose
children aren't there; and then to the people
who are 'like mothers' to other people's
children, even though they have no children of
their own; and finally to everyone who ever had
a mother . . . Oh yes! — nobody leaves our
church without a pot of primroses!

> And he who gives a child a treat
> Makes joy-bells ring in heaven's
> street,

And he who gives a child a home
Builds palaces in Kingdom come,
And she who gives a baby birth
Brings Saviour Christ again to
   Earth.

John Masefield (1878–67)
The Everlasting Mercy (1911)

14 MARCH

Every March our good friend Dr John Tudor
and his team at the Methodist Central Hall,
Westminster, hold a Daffodil Day for members
of the Women's Institute. The whole place is
decorated with daffodils, of course. Over a
thousand women come from all over the
country, in their WI groups, and when the
names are read out, we all cheer. There's a big
tea downstairs — jelly and custard . . . (I promise
you!) And what can I tell you? It's an afternoon
of *love*.

And did those feet, in ancient time
Walk upon England's mountains
   green?
And was the holy Lamb of God
On England's pleasant pastures
   seen?

William Blake
Jerusalem

15 MARCH

Ides of March

Well, all right. Let's have a moment's silence for Julius Caesar on the day he died. Think on — our country would be a very different place today if he hadn't come and seen and conquered — over 2000 years ago! And our great poet, Will Shakespeare, thought he was a hero.

> Cowards die many times before
>   their deaths;
> The valiant never taste of death but
>   once.
> Of all the wonders that I yet have
>   heard,
> It seems to me most strange that
>   men should fear;
> Seeing that death, a necessary end,
> Will come when it will come.
> *William Shakespeare (1564–1616)*

16 MARCH

We do have to put up with some awful weather, don't we? Oh well, they say it's character-forming. Although I can't say that the cold winds are doing much for my character at the moment!

Dirty British coaster with a salt-
caked smoke stack,
Butting through the Channel in the
mad March days,
With a cargo of Tyne coal,
Road-rail, pig-lead,
Firewood, iron-ware and cheap tin
trays.

John Masefield (1878–1967)
Cargoes

17 MARCH

St Patrick's Day, Apostle of Ireland

'St Patrick's Breastplate' is the best known, but
I've discovered that there are other prayers in
the same Irish Celtic 'breastplate' tradition.
Here's part of one for the blessing of a new
home — isn't it nice?

Be Christ's cross on your new
  dwelling,
Be Christ's cross on your new hearth,
Be Christ's cross on your new abode,
Upon your new fire blazing . . .
Each day and each night of your lives,
Each day and each night of your lives.

18 MARCH

We've started work on the *Praise Be!* scripts, for recording next month, and filming the interviews with some of my guests for the programmes. Well, no, I don't really 'interview' them — I drop in for a chat, and have a lovely time . . .

I spent a beautiful day with Paul Heiney at his farm in Suffolk. We sat on hay bales in the evening sunshine, and it was beautiful. You could think you were back a hundred years ago! Paul has all sorts of different animals in his farmyard, like Old MacDonald, and most of them are loved and have names! He also grows all the crops he needs to feed them. He has to work his socks off, but at the end of a warm spring day the sounds of happy, grunting pigs and the smell of sweet hay take a lot of beating!

> To get the whole world out of bed
> And washed, and dressed, and
>   warmed, and fed,
> To work, and back to bed again,
> Believe me, Saul, costs worlds of
>   pain.
>
> *John Masefield (1878–1967)*
> *The Everlasting Mercy (1911)*

19 MARCH

Another happy *Praise Be!* encounter was having tea with the Rt Reverend David Hope, Bishop of London. I mean no disrespect when I say he's what I call a real 'leading man'! He made our tea himself, and wouldn't accept any help, although, between you and me, he'd *bought* the little cakes . . . Well, fair's fair — being a bishop must keep you very busy!

Alleluia, Bread of angels,
Thou on earth our food, our stay;
Alleluia, here the sinful
Flee to thee from day to day;
Intercessor, Friend of sinners,
Earth's Redeemer, plead for me,
Where the songs of all the sinless
Sweep across the crystal sea.
W. Chatterton Dix (1837–98)

20 MARCH

Vernal Equinox

At last the days are as long as the nights, and for the next three months they will stretch out, longer and longer.

In the beginning God created the
  heaven and the earth.
And the earth was without form,
  and void;
and darkness was upon the face of
  the deep.
And the Spirit of God moved upon
  the face of the waters.
And God said, 'Let there be light':
and there was light.

Genesis 1:1–3

21 MARCH

Something I've come to notice over the years
is how spring doesn't arrive all at once. It
unfolds itself gradually, in different colours. At
first it's just something in the air, and perhaps
a few pinpricks of colour, green or purple,
showing through the bare flowerbeds and on
the trees; and tiny white blackthorn flowers in
the bare hedgerows. Then comes what I call the
'yellow' spring. All the yellow crocuses seem to
come out first, before the purple or blue or
white ones, and yellow primroses, and yellow
flowering shrubs, and thousands and thousands
of daffodils.

. . . daffodils,
That come before the swallow
dares, and take

The winds of March with beauty.
William Shakespeare
The Winter's Tale

22 MARCH

I'm never likely to forget the week we played
As you Are in rep. at the Royalty Theatre,
Morecambe. I was cast in the character part of
the mother-in-law, Emma Pearson, a woman of
sixty. I was in my twenties, so my make-up
included rather heavy greasepaint lines and a
paste nose.

When the curtain was about to rise one night,
the buzz went round the company 'George
Formby's in front!' Repertory actors are always
hoping 'big names' will come and see their
shows — it's the only way you can hope to
become a 'big name' yourself.

I was just taking off my paste nose after the
show when I was informed that Mr and Mrs
Formby wanted to meet me. He said he was
going to make a film of *As you Are*, and that he
would like me to repeat my own part in it. He
then said he would arrange for me to go to
Ealing Film Studios for a film test . . . I was
dumbstruck, and they left me standing there in
a trance, my paste nose pointing towards my
left ear.

I gave a great sigh, and as I did so my head
went back and my eyes looked up. I was

standing underneath the 'grave drop'. 'I know *you*, don't I?' the grave drop seemed to say, in our Nev's voice of years ago when we played there as children. Then I cried.

> So many worlds, so much to do,
> So little done, such things to be.
> *Alfred, Lord Tennyson (1809–92)*
> *In Memoriam*

23 MARCH

As we're in the month of the Celtic saints — David and Patrick — here's another of those beautiful, ancient Celtic prayers.

A Good Wish
The good of eye be thine,
The good of liking be thine,
The good of my heart's desire.

The good of sons be thine,
The good of daughters be thine,
The good of the sap of my sense.

The good of sea be thine,
The good of land be thine,
The good of the Prince of heaven.

Another memory: Long after my father left the Royalty Theatre it still continued to play a big part in our lives, and of course, we continued to live next door, at Number 6, Cheapside. One day, when I was in my teens and working as a cashier at the Co-op, the little resident repertory company was presenting a play at the Royalty with a larger cast of artists than they could quite muster, and they asked me 'would I oblige!' Of course I did. And, you might guess, that was the thin end of the wedge, and before long I had joined the company permanently.

The parts I played in those far-off days were very small, so, consequently, I was off-stage more than I was on, but that had its advantages. The dressing rooms were under the stage, our childhood hunting ground, so whilst all the artists with the big parts (pardon the expression!) were acting their socks off overhead, I would wander around my old childhood haunts, happily reminiscing.

> I remember, I remember,
> The house where I was born,
> The little window where the sun
> Came peeping in at morn.
> *Thomas Hood (1799–1845)*

25 MARCH

Lent is forty-six days long, not forty, which you'll know only too well if you've given up meat, chocolates, smoking, or being beastly to everybody . . . But you get it back to forty, if you don't count Sundays. After all, Sunday should always be a day of celebration for Christians, not fasting — because it's the day Jesus rose from the dead. The only trouble is, it's an even harder test of will-power, going back to abstinence on Monday, if you've let rip on Sunday . . .

Forty days and forty nights
Thou wast fasting in the wild;
Forty days and forty nights
Tempted, and yet undefiled:

Shall not we thy sorrows share,
And from earthly joys abstain,
Fasting with unceasing prayer,
Glad with thee to suffer pain?
G.H. Smyttan (1825–70)

26 MARCH

Flicka was a dear little donkey belonging to my friend Liz Barr, who helps me with my books — including this one! Liz and her husband, Andrew, moved from Kent to Scotland, so her two old donkeys, Jacko and Flicka, both nearly thirty years old, went to live at the Donkey Sanctuary in Devon. It was at Liz's suggestion that we filmed there one year, for *Praise Be!*

There I met Elizabeth Svensden and she told me about the work she does to help donkeys all over the world. And the donkeys at the Sanctuary repay her kindness by helping handicapped children, who learn to ride on them. I even got a long-held dream fulfilled, and had a ride in a donkey cart!

Little Flicka, God rest her, has died today. She will have a memorial stone under a plane tree in the Walk of Remembrance at the Donkey Sanctuary. Please say a little prayer for her if you ever happen to be passing . . .

> Fools! For I also had my hour;
> One far fierce hour and sweet:
> There was a shout about my ears,
> And palms before my feet.
>
> G.K. *Chesterton*

27 MARCH

Waking up early on a fine March morning — it's almost impossible *not* to feel a surge of happiness.

> The year's at the spring,
> And day's at the morn;

Morning's at seven;
The hillside's dew-pearled;
The lark's on the wing;
The snail's on the thorn;
God's in his heaven —
All's right with the world!

Robert Browning (1812–89)
Pippa Passes

28 MARCH
British Summer-time

Even though it means getting up an hour earlier, I always look forward to setting the clocks an hour forward in March — the days almost immediately feel longer and lighter. And I *do not* like changing them back again in October, drawing night into the middle of the afternoon!

It may be a bit far-fetched to call 28 March the beginning of British *Summer*-time — but at least it gets our hopes up!

If March comes in like a lion, it
will go out like a lamb.

There's a well-known old show-business saying: 'The show must go on.' People always make rather a joke about it nowadays, and some very highly paid young 'pop' stars of today ignore it completely . . . Nevertheless, most professional artists still feel that they *must* go on — whatever is happening in their personal lives.

All the same there *are* occasions when it seems very hard to go on — the stage I mean — but one does. I recall, very vividly, the day my mother died, in 1942. I was in rep. and, would you believe it, for my first entrance I was attired in black for a funeral, and my opening line was, 'If we're going to mourn the departed, we must do it completely.' The strange thing was that, as I walked on to the stage and said the line, I said it without any additional emotion; in other words, I said it as I had rehearsed it. It was the *rest* of the cast who could hardly speak.

When the final curtain was down, I went to my — shared — dressing room, and my dad was sitting there. 'Hello, Dad! What are you doing here?' I asked, ever so brightly.

'I don't know,' he answered. As we walked home a lump of pain, like a brick, formed under my ribs. It stayed there without changing for weeks.

Then one day, after carefully saving my meat coupons for weeks so that I could give Scottie a mixed grill for his lunch when he arrived home on leave from the RAF, I gazed at the little kidney, the weary sausage and minute piece of steak, and the bit of shrivelled bacon, all huddled together on the plate, and I can remember thinking, 'Oh, he *will* enjoy this!' My anticipation of Scottie's joy was so great that I forgot to use an oven glove to hold the plate. It was red-hot, and I dropped the blasted thing. It fell upside down on a piece of coconut matting! I cried for over an hour. And the brick under my ribs started to dissolve.

My darling Scottie sat at the dining-room table in his RAF uniform, picking coconut matting hairs out of the mutilated offering, and saying, 'Don't cry, love, it's lovely — *really!'* But of course he knew I was crying because I'd lost my mother.

> . . . when I stood forlorn,
> Knowing my heart's best treasure
>   was no more;
> That neither present time, nor years
>   unborn
> Could to my sight that heavenly
>   face restore.
>   *William Wordsworth (1770–1850)*

30 MARCH

One thing you learn as you get older is that there are *always* good people, and reasons for hope, however bad the news is in the papers.

> I have seen flowers come in stony
>   places
> And kind things done by men with
>   ugly faces
> And the gold cup won by the
>   worst horse at the races,
> So I trust, too.
>
>   *John Masefield (1878–1967)*

31 MARCH

The last day of holy March, with its cold winds and sharp frosts mixed with days of surprising warmth and beauty. I'm looking forward to April, May and June, but we mustn't forget how much we owe to the endurance and faith of the Celtic saints who we meet each March.

> Bless to me, O God,
> The earth beneath my foot,
> Bless to me, O God,
> The path whereon I go;
> Bless to me, O God,
> The thing of my desire;
> Thou evermore of evermore,

Bless thou to me my rest.

Bless to me the thing
Whereon is set my mind,
Bless to me the thing
Whereon is set my love;
Bless to me the thing
Whereon is set my hope;
O thou King of kings,
Bless thou to me mine eye!

Celtic journey blessing

APRIL

It's a warm wind, the west wind,
   full of birds' cries;
I never hear the west wind but
   tears are in my eyes,
For it comes from the west lands,
   the old brown hills,
And April's in the westwind, and
   daffodils.
         John Masefield

1 APRIL

All Fools' Day

My mother had a great sense of humour. Well, you have to, don't you, if you're born on 1 April? I know some people who won't even admit to it! Very few days go by when I don't think of my wonderful mother, but 1 April, her birthday, is always an extra remembering.

There's a hymn we get a lot of requests for on *Praise Be!* that still makes me cry, because she chose it for her funeral — 'Lead, kindly Light'.

Lead, kindly Light, amid the
    encircling gloom,
Lead thou me on;
The night is dark, and I am far from
    home;
Lead thou me on.
Keep thou my feet; I do not ask to see
The distant scene; one step enough
    for me.

I was not ever thus, nor prayed that
    thou
Shouldst lead me on;
I loved to choose and see my path;
    but now
Lead thou me on.
I loved the garish day, and, spite of
    fears,

Pride ruled my will: remember not
    past years.

So long thy power hath blest me, sure
    it still
Will lead me on
O'er moor and fen, o'er crag and
    torrent, till
The night is gone,
And with the morn those angel faces
    smile,
Which I have loved long since, and
    lost a while.

J.H. Newman (1801–90)

2 APRIL
—-—

We don't visit the cottage so much in the cold
weather after Christmas, but once April begins,
Scottie and I return with the cuckoo!

Oh! to be in England
Now that April's there,
And whoever wakes in England
Sees, some morning, unaware,
That the lowest boughs and the
    brushwood sheaf
Round the elm-tree bole are in tiny
    leaf,
While the chaffinch sings on the
    orchard bough

In England — now!
                        Robert Browning (1812–89)
                        Home Thoughts from Abroad

3 APRIL

Because the *Praise Be!* team will soon be here, one of the first things to do when we get to the cottage is the spring cleaning!

> Lord of all pots and pans and
> things;
>   since I've no time to be
> a saint by doing lovely things
>   or watching late with thee,
> or dreaming in the dawnlight,
>   or storming heaven's gates,
> make me a saint by getting meals,
>   and washing up the plates.

Anon.
from Short Prayers for the Long Day

4 APRIL

Palm Sunday

Every year I come home from church with a palm cross, and I put it on a shelf — and now I've got so many!

And when they drew nigh unto
Jerusalem, and were come to
Bethphage, unto the mount of
Olives, then sent Jesus two
disciples,
Saying unto them, 'Go into the
village over against you, and
straightaway ye shall find an ass
tied, and a colt with her: loose
them, and bring them unto me.
And if any man say ought unto
you, ye shall say, "The Lord hath
need of them"; and straightway he
will send them.'
    . . . and the disciples went, and
did as Jesus commanded them,
    And brought the ass, and the
colt, and put on them their clothes,
and they set him thereon.
And a very great multitude spread
their garments in the way; others
cut down branches from the trees,
and strewed them in the way.
    And the multitudes that went
before, and that followed, cried,
saying, 'Hosanna to the Son of
David: Blessed is he that cometh in
the name of the Lord; Hosanna in
the highest.'
And when he was come into
Jerusalem, all the city was moved,
saying, 'Who is this?'

And the multitude said, 'This is
Jesus the prophet of Nazareth of
Galilee.'

Matthew 21:1–3, 6–11

5 APRIL

Scottie and I usually get seized with gardening
fever at this time of year. Have you ever read
The Gardener's Year by Karel Capek? It's full of
jokes, although the author manages to impart
a lot of knowledge and practical information
between laughs. Here is his idea of a gardener's
'prayer'.

O Lord, grant that in some way it
may rain every day, say from
midnight until three o'clock in the
morning, but, you see, it must be
gentle and warm so that it can soak
in; grant that at the same time it
would not rain on campion,
alyssum, helianthemum, lavender,
and the others which you in your
infinite wisdom know are drought-
loving plants — I will write their
names on a bit of paper if you like
— and grant that the sun may shine
the whole day long, but not
everywhere (not for instance on
spiraea, or on gentian, plaintain lily

and rhododendron) — and not too much; that there may be plenty of dew and little wind, enough worms, no plant-lice and snails, no mildew, and that once a week thin liquid manure and guano may fall from heaven. Amen.

6 APRIL

Another of Karel Capek's stories is about an American millionaire visiting an English garden.

The American said to the owner:
'Sir, I will pay you anything you like if you will reveal to me by what method such a perfect, even, level, fresh, everlasting — in short, such an English lawn as your is made.'

'That's quite simple,' said the English squire. 'The soil must be well and deeply dug, it must be fertile and porous, not heavy or thin; then it must be well levelled so that it is like a table; after that you sow the seed and roll the ground well; then you water it daily, and when the grass has grown up you mow it week after

week; you collect the cut grass with
sweepers and roll the lawn; you
must water, sprinkle, wet and spray
it daily; and if you do this for 300
years, you will have as good a lawn
as mine!'

Karel Capek
The Gardener's Year

7 APRIL

In Spalding, in Lincolnshire, they have a big
Tulip Parade early in April, and thousands of
visitors come to see it. The flat, fertile fenland
around Spalding is ideal for bulbs, and as you
drive through endless horizons of yellow and
scarlet on a warm April day, you can easily see
why it's known as Little Holland. As well as the
great fields of bulbs, every little cottage garden
has its own speciality tulip, and travelling along
the straight fen roads, with dykes at either side,
you squeeze past lorry after lorry loaded high
with different coloured flowers.

In the big fields the tulip heads are cut off as
soon as they bloom, in order to produce richer
bulbs to sell to us for our gardens. But please
don't think that more than a million beautiful
tulip flowers are allowed to go to waste . . . Far
from it. They are taken in to town and
individually stuck on to hundreds of
magnificent floats for the parade, to be sat on

by scantily clad girls and the Tulip Time Queen, and accompanied by marching bands and drum majorettes and all the things that go with a proper Carnival parade.

> When it's spring again
> I'll bring again
> Tulips from Amsterdam.
> *Max Bygraves' song*

8 APRIL

Today is Maundy Thursday . . . *this* year. Of course, by the time anyone reads this it won't be a Thursday, and probably nowhere near Easter . . . But as far as I'm concerned, today Her Majesty is down at Westminster Abbey doling out the Maundy Money, and in cathedrals all over the world oil is being blessed which will be used to anoint new priests being ordained in the next year. In the evening bishops everywhere will be kneeling to wash the feet of twelve chosen parishioners — although you can be sure that those feet will have been thoroughly scrubbed and probably *boiled* by said parishioners prior to arriving for the ceremony!

> Jesus knowing that the Father had given all things into his hands, and that he was come from God, and

94

went to God; He riseth from
supper, and laid aside his garments;
and took a towel, and girded
himself.
After that he poureth water into a
basin, and began to wash the
disciples' feet, and to wipe them
with the towel wherewith he was
girded.

John 13:3–5

9 APRIL

— —

Good Friday

And when they were come unto a
place called Golgotha, that is to say,
the place of the skull,
They gave him vinegar to drink
mingled with gall: and when he
had tasted thereof, he would not
drink.
And they crucified him, and parted
his garments, casting lots: that it
might be fulfilled which was
spoken by the prophet, 'They
parted my garments among them,
and upon my vesture did they cast
lots.'
And sitting down they watched him
there;
And set up over his head his
accusation written, THIS IS THE KING

Then were there two thieves
crucified with him, one on the
right hand, and another on the left.
Matthew 27:33–38

10 APRIL
—●—

The weather is cold, wet and misty. Sometimes
it can be boiling hot over the Easter weekend;
sometimes it can snow. This year it's wet and
overcast, with rather a chilly wind. That hasn't
stopped multitudes of primroses, violets,
periwinkles and crocuses from opening up — in
fact everything's rather early — but on our walk
this afternoon the birds weren't singing much.
Too cold!

> Yesterday there was deep snow,
> though the trees are in bloom.
> Plum trees and cherry trees full of
> blossom look so queer in a snow
> landscape, their lovely foamy
> fullness goes a sort of pinky drab,
> and the snow looks fiendish in its
> cold incandescence. I hated it
> violently.
> *D.H. Lawrence (1885–1930)*
> *Letter, April 1918 (Berkshire)*

11 APRIL

I've never forgotten — and never will forget —
Easter Sunday a few years ago, when Jan and I
got up very early in the morning to go to the
churchyard for the Easter vigil. You can tell
how early we were, because it was still dark.
Roger, our vicar, had a fire blazing in the
churchyard, and we all sang a hymn and then
we prayed. Then we just waited.

For a few moments there was nothing but
darkness and silence, and then, as the very first
pale glimmer of the rising sun appeared — every
bird in Sussex started singing.

Jesus Christ is risen today. Alleluia!

12 APRIL

On Bank Holidays Jan sometimes likes to
entertain friends to lunch 'American style': that
means everyone is asked to bring a different
course. Someone brings a starter, someone else
— vegetables, various people might bring
salads, someone brings a fish course, others
might bring wine or a fruit cup, several people
bring different — and usually absolutely
gorgeous — puddings.

It's great, because it means that the hosts can
look forward to everyone coming, without
having to slave all morning to provide all the

food, or worrying about whether they've done enough. There's always more than enough, and it's all delicious!

> Oh, I get by with a little help from my friends!
> *John Lennon and Paul McCartney*
> *Song, 1967*

13 APRIL
——

The daffodils were all out so early this year, they're almost over in the South. Have you ever read *Dorothy* Wordsworth's account of the day she and her brother saw the daffodils that inspired his famous poem?

> When we were in the woods
> beyond Gowbarrow park we saw a
> few daffodils close to the water-
> side. We fancied that the lake had
> floated the seeds ashore, and the
> little colony had so sprung up. But
> as we went along there were more
> and yet more; and at last, under the
> boughs of the trees, we saw that
> there was a long belt of them along
> the shore, about the breadth of a
> country turnpike road. I never saw
> daffodils so beautiful. They grew
> among the mossy stones about

them; some rested their heads upon
these stones as on a pillow for
weariness; and the rest tossed and
reeled and danced, and seemed as if
they were verily laughing with the
wind, that blew upon them over
the lake; they looked so gay, ever
glancing, ever changing. This wind
blew directly over the lake to them.
There was here and there a little
knot, and a few stragglers a few
yards higher up; but they were so
few as not to disturb the simplicity,
unity, and life of the one busy
highway.

Dorothy Wordsworth (1771–1855)
Letter, April 1802 (Westmorland)

14 APRIL

And here, just to remind you, is her brother's
poem on the same scene.

> I wandered lonely as a cloud
> That floats on high o'er vales and
>   hills
> When all at once I saw a crowd,
> A host, of golden daffodils;
> Beside the lake, beneath the trees,
> Fluttering and dancing in the
>   breeze.

99

Continuous as the stars that shine
And twinkle on the milky way,
They stretch'd in never-ending line
Along the margin of a bay:
Ten thousand saw I at a glance
Tossing their heads in sprightly
    dance.

The waves beside them danced, but
    they
Out-did the sparkling waves in
    glee:-
A poet could not but be gay,
In such a jocund company!
I gazed — and gazed — but little
    thought
What wealth to me the show had
    brought:

For oft, when on my couch I lie
In vacant or in pensive mood,
They flash upon that inward eye
Which is the bliss of solitude;
And then my heart with pleasure
    fills,
And dances with the daffodils.
          William Wordsworth (1770–1850)

15 APRIL

In many London streets the trees are covered in
pink and white blossom. It makes me smile to

see them — they look like gnarled old men
wearing their wives' Easter bonnets for a lark!
It's only seeing them in town that makes them
seem like that — cherry trees are beautiful really.

> Loveliest of trees, the cherry now
> Is hung with bloom along the
>   bough,
> And stands about the woodland
>   ride
> Wearing white for Eastertide.
> > *A.E. Housman (1859–1936)*

16 APRIL

I've found another of those 'breastplate'
prayers.

> Christ's cross over this face, and
> thus over my ear.
> Christ's cross over this eye. Christ's
> cross over this nose.
> Christ's cross to accompany me
> before. Christ's cross to accompany
> me behind. Christ's cross to meet
> every difficulty both on hollow and
> hill.
> Christ's cross eastwards facing me.
> Christ's cross back towards the
> sunset. In the north, in the south,
> increasingly may Christ's cross

straightway be.
Christ's cross up to broad heaven.
Christ's cross down to earth. Let
no evil or hurt come to my body
or my soul. Christ's cross over me
as I sit. Christ's cross over me as I
lie. Christ's cross be all my strength
until we reach the King of heaven.
From the top of my head to the
nail of my foot, O Christ, against
every danger I trust in the
protection of the cross.
Till the day of my death, going
into this clay, I shall draw without
— Christ's cross over this face.

17 APRIL
—-—

Thought for the day:

> You see things; and you say 'Why?'
> But I dream things that never were;
> and I say 'Why not?'
> *George Bernard Shaw (1856–1950)*
> *Back to Methuselah (1921)*

18 APRIL
—-—

The Sunday after Easter is called Low Sunday
— and the congregation in church is often rather

thin on the ground. I hope there will be plenty of people watching the first episode of *Praise Be!* tonight!

Reasons for Not Going to Church: No. 2

A lady and her husband have left their church because their minister:
'. . . though he is no doubt a good man and very earnest, is so tedious. Just for example, he was preaching two weeks ago, or was it three? — I am really so bad at remembering dates, and so was poor Mamma — perhaps it was four, I'm not sure, but I'm pretty certain it was some time or other within the last month — or two months. But do you know, his text was "eternal glory" or something or other like that, and he preached on it for fifty minutes! . . . You don't mean to say that's five striking? I didn't think it was near four! How time does fly when one is interested!'

The Morning Watch, April 1905

19 APRIL

Here is my haiku for April.

> In the garden full
> Of daffodils — a film crew!
> Praise Be! It's April.

Are you getting the hang of these now?

20 APRIL

I think I'll go for a little saunter in the garden today, and pick some primroses for the kitchen table — where Scottie and I eat most of our meals.

> What brings joy to the heart is not
> so much the friend's gift as the
> friend's love.
> *St Aelred of Rievaulx (1109–1167)*

21 APRIL

It's the Queen's birthday today. They played the National Anthem on the radio this morning, but I don't remember a time when the press and politicians, who ought to know better, have been so continually disloyal or made life so unhappy for the Queen. But we love you, so a very happy birthday, Your Majesty!

God save our gracious Queen,
Long live our noble Queen,
God save the Queen.
Send her victorious,
Happy and glorious,
Long to reign over us:
God save the Queen.

Anon.

22 APRIL

I don't know what anybody's going to make of a new project I'm just embarking on for the BBC. It's to be called *Thora on the Broad and Narrow* — but even I don't really understand what it's all about!

I've been shown this wonderful Victorian poster, called The Broad and Narrow Way. It shows two paths — one leading to hell and damnation, and the other leading to heaven. The path to hell is broad and wide, and lined with theatres and public houses, full of people behaving badly. The other path is steep and narrow and tortuous, and has a church and a Sunday School beside it. All along the two paths are little Bible texts.

Well, I dare say I shall be somewhat wiser after I've had a meeting with Bryan Izzard, the Producer.

Enter ye in at the strait gate: for
wide is the gate, and broad is the
way, that leadeth to destruction,
and many there be which go in
thereat:
Because strait is the gate, and
narrow is the way, which leadeth
unto life, and few there be that
find it.

Matthew 7:13–14

23 APRIL

St George's Day

If we're down at the cottage I always go out on
St George's Day to see if I can see any sign of
the first swallows and house martins arriving.
And I nearly always do — usually just one. I
think they send out a 'scout' as an advance
guard, to check whether all the old nesting sites
are still there. They have a quick buzz round and
then fly back to the others, who are coming on
more slowly, and say, 'It's all right! Everything
is just as it was!'

Sometimes a few weeks may go by before we
see any more; then they all arrive together and
start building and rebuilding their old nests.

Yes, the sparrow hath found an
house, and the swallow a nest for

self, where she may lay her young.
Psalm 84:3

24 APRIL

When Jan was a little girl we were living in another cottage in the country, and there was a house martin's nest under the eaves. I don't know whether you've ever been close enough to observe a house martin's nest, but I'm here to tell you, that when the young birds are old enough to start learning to fly, your heart is in your mouth! They look so frightened, and cling to the outside of the nest, while the parents fly backwards and forwards, trying to encourage them to take off. Jan had me and Scottie and her Nanny outside in the garden for hours one year, holding out the four corners of a big blanket as a safety net!

Father, hear the prayer we offer:
Not for ease that prayer shall be,
But for strength that we may ever
Live our lives courageously.
Mrs L.M. Willis (1864)

25 APRIL

— —

Anzac Day

Today is Anzac Day, the equivalent of our Remembrance Day, in the lands beneath the Southern Cross — Australia and New Zealand. I have such happy memories of both countries, having been 'on tour' there several times, and I'd love to go again . . . Who knows — perhaps we shall!

I've been very thrilled in recent years to receive letters from both countries, because now they even get *Praise Be!* over there! Oh the wonders of modern science!

> The sun that bids us rest is waking
> Our brethren 'neath the western
> sky,
> And hour by hour fresh lips are
> making
> Thy wondrous doings heard on
> high.
>
> *J. Ellerton (1826–93)*
> *'The day thou gavest, Lord, is ended'*

26 APRIL

— —

Once on *Praise Be!* we visited Spring Harvest, a Christian festival held every spring at a holiday camp in Minehead. I remember interviewing the young hymn-writer, Graham Kendrick, who writes hymns for a new generation of Christians. They are so good that one has even got into the *Songs of Praise* Top Ten Favourite Hymns.

Have you ever been to Spring Harvest? It's full of teenagers. And do you know what they do? They go into different circus tents — I was in the Big Top with Graham Kendrick — to listen to speakers who teach them about Christianity. They study the Bible; they celebrate the Gospel; they learn new dances; they laugh a lot, and sometimes they cry; they make new friends; they have a smashing time!

> Shine, Jesus, shine,
> Fill this land with the Father's
>   glory;
> Blaze, Spirit, blaze,
> Set our hearts on fire,
> Flow, river, flow,
> Flood the nations with grace and
>   mercy;
> Send forth your word, Lord,
> And let there be light.
>
> *Graham Kendrick (1988)*

27 APRIL

The first two *Praise Be!* programmes have gone out and more letters are beginning to arrive, mainly from nice people who want to tell me how much they are enjoying it, and a few from people who want to know if there is still time to request a hymn. As we finished recording all the programmes over a week ago, there's no chance of that. Fortunately I know in advance that such letters will arrive, so I always put into the script around programme three that I'm sorry, but people who have only just written are too late. Never mind — there's always next year — D.V. — God willing!

> This is the day which the Lord hath made; we will rejoice and be glad in it.
>
> *Psalm 118:24*

28 APRIL

A Christian writer who has given me great pleasure in recent years is Adrian Plass, who lives not far from us in Sussex. Here's a typical extract from his book *View from a Bouncy Castle*.

> In the year when Katy became three, I strolled into the garden one sparkling April morning, to find my diminutive daughter pushing one arm up as far as it would go towards the sky. In her outstretched hand was a single bluebell, newly

picked from the border beside the lawn. As she offered her flower to the shining early sun, she identified it with loud ecstasy. 'DAFFODIL!!' she shouted, 'DAFFODI-I-ILL!!'

I am as tediously obsessed with accuracy as most parents. I corrected her gently. 'No, darling,' I said, 'it's a bluebell.'

Not one inch did she reduce the length of her stretching arm, not one decibel did she lower her volume: 'BLUEBELL!!' she shouted, 'BLUEBE-E-ELL!!' Katy's joy was in being part of the morning and having a beautiful flower, not in anything so trivial as being right. My pedantic correction didn't change anything important.

If only those of us who are Christians were more like Katy in the garden . . . 'YOU HAVE TO SPEAK IN TONGUES TO BE A CHRISTIAN!!' one of us might shout out ecstatically.

'No, you don't', God might correct us gently.
'YOU DON'T HAVE TO SPEAK IN TONGUES TO BE A CHRISTIAN!!' we would shout with undiminished joy.

Adrian Plass

29 APRIL

— —

On a really warm April morning you sometimes find last year's butterflies waking up and jostling with the bees for a place in the sun among the primroses. You can always tell if they are old butterflies, because their wings look a bit frayed round the edges!

> The toad beneath the harrow knows
> Exactly where each tooth-point
>   goes;
> The butterfly upon the road
> Preaches contentment to that toad.
>   *Rudyard Kipling (1865–1936)*
>   *Departmental Ditties*

30 APRIL

— —

Well, I know a little bit more about *Thora on the Broad and Narrow* now. Bryan Izzard, the Producer, is going to build a stage set at Pinewood Studios, reproducing the Victorian poster he showed me. Pinewood! What a wonderful homecoming that will be! I couldn't tell you exactly how many films I made there for Rank Films after the war. Sadly there are few — if any — films being made there now. It's nearly all 'ads' these days.

For this series I have to dress up as a Victorian Sunday School teacher, and each week I have to take a group of choirboys, the Angel Voices, along the right way — the narrow way. But they will keep wanting to get over onto the broad way. I think that's it. I'll keep you informed when I know more!

Hi diddle dee dee (an actor's life for me)!

Ned Washington (1940)

MAY

'Tomorrow you will learn "Here we
come gathering nuts in May", said
Jonathan Rabbit, 'and you must
choose whom you will have for your
nuts in May.'
Alison Uttley
Fuzzypeg goes to School

1 MAY

It's many years ago since I was Morecambe's May Queen, but — you can bet — I've still got the photograph! It may seem a quaint custom to young people today, but I'm here to tell you, for a little girl of eight or nine to be crowned Queen of the May in her home town is one of those wonderful days that you never forget for the rest of your life.

> You must wake and call me early,
>   call me early, Mother dear;
> Tomorrow'll be the happiest time of
>   all the glad New-year;
> Of all the glad New-year, Mother,
>   the maddest merriest day;
> For I'm to be Queen o' the May,
> Mother, I'm to be Queen o' the
>   May.
>   *Alfred, Lord Tennyson (1809–92)*

2 MAY

It was very bleak this morning, after a few days of lovely spring weather. At the end of April or the beginning of May, if you get a dark, cold spell when the blackthorn is in full flower, they call it 'the blackthorn winter'.

A very cold morning — hail and
snow showers all day . . . we . . .
walked backwards and forwards in
Brothers Wood. William tired
himself with seeking an epithet for
the cuckoo.

Dorothy Wordsworth
May 1802 (Westmorland)

3 MAY

Scottie's and my happy wedding anniversary
day. Fifty-six years . . . And yes, we would do
it all again!

Marriage is like twirling a baton,
turning handsprings, or eating with
chopsticks; it looks so easy till you
try it!

Helen Rowland (1876–1945)

4 MAY

The best joy to come out of Scottie's and my
marriage has been our beautiful daughter, Jan.
I won't sing her praises too much, because
you'll think it's just a mother's prejudice! But
even now, when her own children are almost
grown up, she's still the same generous
daughter who plans lovely surprises for her

'aged parents'!

For instance, a few years ago yesterday was our Golden Wedding Anniversary. Jan hired a painted canal barge for the day on the Regent's Canal as a complete surprise to us, and invited all our dearest friends to join us there for a floating lunch. It was the best present we could ever have had — although the two airline tickets to Florida for a holiday with her and William, which were enclosed in our card, were very acceptable too . . . I had been wondering why she insisted we needed our passports to travel on a canal barge!

A gift she gave me one Mothering Sunday, which I shall always treasure, is a beautiful picture of a flower embroidered with the words:

> God couldn't be everywhere —
> That's why he created mothers!

5 MAY

Do you remember the childrens' stories of *Little Grey Rabbit* by Alison Uttley? Well I still enjoy reading them! Here's part of *Fuzzypeg goes to School*. After being summoned to school by the ringing of harebells, three little hedgehogs arrive out of breath and rather late for their first day at school.

. . . The door swung open, and they entered a room, whose walls were made of closely woven blackberry bushes and wild roses, whose floor was the soft fragrant turf of the pasture, starred with wild thyme, and blue milk-wort, and sweet clover, growing over it like a pattern in a carpet. The ceiling of the schoolroom was the blue sky, where the sun was now shining, so that the little hedgehogs saw their shadows at their sides as they walked shyly across the room to Old Jonathan.

'Benjamin Hedgehog. Timothy Hedgehog. Fuzzypeg Hedgehog,' said he, writing their names on a rose-leaf, in squiggly letters. 'Each of you is "A diller, a dollar, A ten-o'clock scholar." Remember that school begins at nine o'clock, and don't be late!'

Alison Uttley
Fuzzypeg goes to School

6 MAY

I loved my own school days. I was an average scholar, but I've always been quick at mental arithmetic and — though I don't want to sound swanky — I've always had neat handwriting. I can still remember nearly all the words of the poems and songs we were taught at school. Above all, I'll never forget the kindness and happiness of those days at Miss Nelson's, with all my classmates.

When I first left school, I was fourteen . . . And on the first day of the next term, while my friends were all walking along the road back to school, I stood at home gazing forlornly out of the window, wearing my old school gym-slip, white blouse and school tie! What a pathetic sight! My wonderful mother came in, and seeing my look of woe, paused only for a moment before she said, 'Get your satchel and run along and see if Miss Nelson will have you back for another term!'

I flew! Miss Nelson was still greeting all her pupils as they filed in for assembly. 'Good morning, Madge. Good morning, Norah. Good morning, Ada. Good morning, Thora . . . *Thora?* . . . I thought you'd left school,' she said.

'May I come back for another term?' I asked.

'With pleasure,' she said (she was quite moved).

'It's nice to see you back, Thora.'

I'm here to tell you that I've never sung 'Holy, holy, holy!' with more gusto than I did that morning!

Holy, Holy, Holy! Lord God
almighty!
Early in the morning our song shall
rise to thee;
Holy, Holy, Holy! merciful and
mighty!
God in three Persons, blessed
Trinity!
                    Bishop R. Heber (1733–1826)

7 MAY

––

William Blake was the sort of person who
could never look at a tree, or anything in nature,
without seeing choirs of angels.

'What,' it will be questioned, 'when
the sun rises, do you not see a
round disc of fire somewhat like a
guinea?' 'O no, no, I see an
innumerable company of the
heavenly host crying, "Holy, Holy,
Holy is the Lord God Almighty."'
                    William Blake (1757–1827)
                    A Vision of the Last Judgement

– –

Julian of Norwich

Six hundred years ago Julian of Norwich lived
in an anchorage — but Julian wasn't a sailor, or
even a man; and *her* 'anchorage' was nowhere
near Norwich harbour — it had nothing to do
with boats! Julian was an anchoress, and her
anchorage was a small cell 'anchored' to the side
of a church in Norwich and it was where the
anchoress — or anchorite, if it were a man —
would live and never leave.

The cell would have had three windows. One
opening on to the church, so she could hear
Mass and receive the sacrament. A second
window would have opened onto an inner
room, so that a servant could bring food and
clean clothes, and take out the slops. And the
third window, curtained by a black cloth with
a white cross in the middle, would have opened
onto the street, so the anchoress could look out
at the bustling world outside, and talk to the
people who came to ask her advice and help.

It was an entirely selfless life, and she herself
said:

> Then shall you soon forget me,
> who am of no account.
> And do so, so that I shall not
> hinder you.

Julian of Norwich

9 MAY

Julian *was* forgotten — completely — for 600 years! No one knows where she came from, when she died or where she is buried.

She had written a book, called *Revelations of Divine Love*, but that was also lost. And then, and this is almost like a miracle, her book was rediscovered — *600* years later. It was first published just twenty years ago, on 8 May 1973. And now Julian speaks to us again, like a voice straight from heaven.

> You would know our Lord's
> meaning in this thing? Know it
> well. Love was his meaning. Who
> showed it you? Love. What did he
> show you? Love. Why did he show
> it? For love. Hold on to this and
> you will know and understand love
> more and more. But you will not
> know or learn anything else — ever!

Julian of Norwich
Revelations of Divine Love
trans. Clifton Wolters

10 MAY

Julian's cell was pulled down at the Reformation. The church, with its little Saxon tower, survived, but then it was badly damaged when it received a direct hit in an air raid in 1942. But thanks to the inspiration and work of the sisters of the Community of All Hallows, Ditchingham — the next-door neighbours — it has been restored. Julian's cell has been rebuilt, and become a wonderful place of prayer and pilgrimage.

On one occasion the good Lord said, 'Everything is going to be all right.' On another, 'You will see for yourself that every sort of thing will be all right.' In these two sayings the soul discerns various meanings.

One is that he wants us to know that not only does he care for great and noble things, but equally for little and small, lowly and simple things as well. This is his meaning: '*Everything* will be all right.' We are to know that the least thing will not be forgotten.

Julian of Norwich
Revelations of Divine Love
trans. Clifton Wolters

– –

You're probably thinking, 'Thora's very knowledgable about all this . . . I never had her down as a clever head!' And you would be right! I'm not. But do you remember that I visited the Community of All Hallows, Ditchingham on *Praise Be!*?

I'll freely admit that my real reason for going there was not because of Julian of Norwich, or her book, but because I have had so much pleasure from another little book, written by Sister Maud CAH, called . . . *Tailwags!*

Here is one of Sister Maud's 'Tailwags' — which were all written between her eightieth and ninetieth birthdays.

> 'Only the tail-end of life is left,' I
>   said;
> And into my head
> A thought came out of the blue,
> A thought from you —
> 'But that is the cheery end,' you
>   said.
> 'So see
> That you use it for me.'
> And I said, 'Amen,' and raised my
>   head.
> 'I will glorify God with a wag,' I
>   said.
>
> *Sister Maud CAH*
> *Tailwag No. 1*

12 MAY

— —

When you visit the Community of All Hallows — and I'm here to tell you that if you do it will be all joy — you'll probably notice that animals play a very big part in the sisters' life. There's always a cat somewhere nearby, staring at you from some sunny window seat. And there are goats and bees, and a hen which lays very blue eggs. In fact, they did me a great honour before I left — they named the hen which lays blue eggs 'Thora' after me!

> All creatures their creator bless
> And worship him in holiness.
> *W.H. Draper (1855–1933)*
> *'All creatures of our God and King'*
> *based on St Francis of Assisi: Canticles*
> *of the Sun*

13 MAY

— —

We're all hard at work on *Thora on the Broad and Narrow*. By jingo — I've got a lot of words to learn! I thought I'd just be introducing a few items — but I appear to be in every scene! Well, I've never been afraid of hard work, and one of the great pleasures for me is revisiting the old J. Arthur Rank film studios at Pinewood, so full of memories.

There's a connection between Pinewood and religion, too, which I'm going to mention in one of the programmes: J. Arthur Rank was a strong Methodist, and so he started a company especially to make religious films. He experimented with special ones to be shown in cinemas on Sundays, and brought out of retirement an old silent film actor called Stewart Rome, who called himself Dr Goodfellow. He used to lean over a farm gate and tell the audience what to do next week, and what to think about . . . At Edgware one Sunday night the audience started to throw things at the screen — so that's when they decided to stop 'Thought for the Week'!

I say! I hope nobody throws things at their television screens when *Thora on the Broad and Narrow* comes on!

No burden is too heavy when
Christ is with us.

14 MAY

If we leave London late and arrive down at the cottage after dark, when Scottie turns off the engine there's a deep, warm silence, the country smell of freshly cut grass, and, if we are very, very lucky, a nightingale will be singing. It's the loveliest sound in all the world.

This is the weather the cuckoo
    likes,
    And so do I;
When showers betumble the
    chestnut spikes,
    And nestlings fly:
And the little brown nightingale
    bills his best,
And they sit outside at 'The
    Travellers' Rest'.
                        Thomas Hardy (1840–1928)
                                        Weathers

---

15 MAY

I think May, my birth month, is the month
when I'm always at my happiest.

When the present has latched its
    postern behind my tremulous stay,
And the May month flaps its glad
    green leaves like wings,
Delicate-filmed as new-spun silk,
    will the neighbours say,
'He was a man who used to notice
    such things'?
                        Thomas Hardy (1840–1928)
                                        Weathers

16 MAY

--

I can't compete with Thomas Hardy, my favourite poet, but here goes with my May haiku.

Shrubbery nestlings
Merrily twitter. Somewhere
A cuckoo's calling.

17 MAY

--

There will be a regular spot on *Thora on the Broad and Narrow* when I chat to Carlo Curly, 'the Pavarotti of the organ', as he's sometimes known. We'll talk about music and hymns, old and new — you know, things like 'Does the Devil have all the best tunes?' I'm looking forward to it. There'll be no script — it'll all be 'ad lib', and Carlo will probably do a tarradiddle on the organ keys. And now I've met him, I'm here to tell you — there won't be any problem about awkward silences!

The scene was one I'll ne'er forget,
    as long as I may live,
And just to see it o'er again
    all earthly wealth I'd give,
The congregation, all amaz'd,
    the preacher old and grey,
The organ and the organist,
    who volunteer'd to play.

18 MAY

— —

I try to give Christian Aid Week a mention most years on *Praise Be!* because of the great work they do.

One year I visited the Brixton headquarters of Christian Aid, and talked to one of the secretaries. Diane said that all the statistical facts and figures, and the millions of pounds that are forever being appealed for, could be a bit off-putting. But when the field workers came back to the office from abroad to make their reports, and they talked about their work; and she heard their stories about villages struggling to survive; and real people, and children, with names and personalities who they had met and come to know, and for whom the help we send can be the difference between life and death . . . then it all seemed worthwhile.

. . . he saw a large crowd; and he took
pity on them because they were like
sheep without a shepherd, and he set
himself to teach them at some length.
   By now it was getting very late, and
his disciples came up to him and said,
'This is a lonely place and it is getting
very late, so send them away, and they
can go to the farms

and villages round about, to buy
themselves something to eat.' He
replied, 'Give them something to eat
yourselves.'

Mark 6:34–37 (Jerusalem Bible)

19 MAY

At this time of year, it's not only Christian Aid
collectors who will be leaving envelopes for us
to put our donations in. May seems to be the
favourite month for all sorts of charities to do
their door-to-door collecting. It's a big job, and
needs a lot of volunteers.

I'm afraid I'm as guilty as anyone of getting
a bit fed up by the time the fifth or sixth
envelope drops through our letter-box in the
space of two weeks, asking us to please be
generous. It's not always easy, but I think it's
important to try *not* to feel irritated, even if you
are already giving a lot away to charities of your
own choosing. But when there's a knock on the
door, and you see the kind, tired face of the
volunteer collector, who will have been to at
least twenty or thirty other houses already that
evening — it's not so very difficult to pop a
pound, or fifty p., into the envelope with a
friendly smile, is it?'

Then cherish pity, lest you drive an
angel from your door.

William Blake
Holy Thursday

20 MAY

Ascension Day

In one village in Kent, Goudhurst, not very far
from us, the choir sometimes climbs the church
tower to serenade the Ascension Day dawn
with a hymn. They were there one year, on a
pouring wet morning, with mackintosh hats
and torches, singing their hearts out, only just
audible from below where the Morris Men
were greeting the dawn with their Ascension
Day dance. Through the village streamed the
early morning commuters in their cars — I
wonder if any of them heard the beautiful
words the choir were singing?

Hail the day that sees him rise
To his throne beyond the skies;
Christ, the Lamb for sinners given,
Enters now the highest heaven!
Alleluia!

See! the heaven its Lord receives,
Yet he loves the earth he leaves;
Though returning to his throne,

Still he calls mankind his own.
Alleluia!

Lord, though parted from our
    sight,
Far beyond the starry height,
Grant our hearts may thither rise,
Seeking thee beyond the skies.
Alleluia!

Charles Wesley (1707–88)

21 MAY

The Church of Scotland holds its annual
General Assembly in Edinburgh this week.
They debate Christian faith and life, and make
decisions about how the Church of Scotland's
money and resources should be spent or saved
over the next year. The Lord High Com-
missioner will come to observe the pro-
ceedings, representing Her Majesty the Queen,
who sometimes comes in person.

Billy Graham addressed the Assembly in
1991, and in 1992, shortly after he was released,
Terry Waite came to tell them of his experiences
as a hostage in Beirut for five years. That great,
kindly giant told them his story, and it was soon
clear that the terrible ordeal hadn't destroyed
his spirit — or his sense of humour. He told
them about a very small girl with saucer eyes
who, after staring at him for a long time, had

come up and asked, 'Were you *really* an ostrich for five years?'

22 MAY

Jan and William recently broke some news to us. They are in the process of selling the Mill House Estate, so Scottie and I are now in the middle of packing up everything in the cottage. They feel the Mill House, with all its land, is too big for the two of them now that William is semi-retired and the children are at university in America. So they have been looking for, and have now found, another house — still in Sussex, but smaller and with less land to look after.

It all makes very good sense . . . but oh! how we shall all miss the village.

> There is nothing permanent —
> except change.
> *Heraclitus (540–475 BC)*

23 MAY

It's the last *Praise Be!* on television tonight. I always feel a bit sad when the last one goes out — I get such a lot of pleasure from doing them. I usually end by saying, 'Goodbye and God bless you. I'll be back next year — D.V. — God willing!'

That's a more carefully thought out sentence than you might suppose. Seventeen years ago, I would have signed off each Sunday by saying to the viewers, 'Goodbye and God bless. I'll be back next week.' But I received a stern letter from a gentleman viewer saying that I should always add 'D.V.' — in case I'm *not* back next Sunday! And several other letters arrived saying, 'Don't say "God bless", Thora. Say "God bless you"!' So I do!

> God be with you till we meet
>   again;
> When life's perils thick confound
>   you,
> Put his arm unfailing round you:
> God be with you till we meet
>   again.
> *Jeremiah Eames Rankin (1824–1904)*

24 MAY

Ever since my visit to Ditchingham, the lovely Mother Superior, Sister Pamela, has kept in touch and sends me news. I know she remembers me in her prayers, as I do her and all the sisters of the Community of All Hallows in mine.

Here's another beautiful passage from Julian of Norwich's book.

And he showed me more, a little thing, the size of a hazel-nut, on the palm of my hand, round like a ball. I looked at it thoughtfully and wondered, 'What is this?'

And the answer came, 'It is all that is made.' I marvelled that it continued to exist and did not suddenly disintegrate; it was so small. And again my mind supplied the answer, 'It exists, both now and for ever, because God loves it.'

Julian of Norwich
Revelations of Divine Love
trans. Clifton Wolters

25 MAY

The woods near the cottage have a blue carpet. One year, I was doing some weeding at the front, when I heard Jan's car crunching on the gravel. She called out, 'Can you come with me, Mummy? It'll only take a minute.' So I got into the car and we drove off, out of the gate, left into the lane, and on for a couple of miles, until we stopped by a gate leading into the woods. I hadn't asked her where we were going, and now we were there I didn't have to. The entire floor of the wood was the deepest, richest blue you ever saw. You couldn't have squeezed in one more bluebell.

. . . to Combe Wood to see and
gather bluebells, which we did, but
fell in blue-handed with a
gamekeeper, which is a humbling
thing to do . . .

> *Gerard Manley Hopkins (1844–89)*
> *May 1874 (Surrey)*

26 MAY

Another birthday looms. I used to swank at
school that my mother's birthday was in April,
my own in May, my dad's in June, my sister
Olga's in July and my brother Neville's in
August. That statement was always received
with open-mouthed amazement, and many
times I was requested to 'Go on, Hirdie, and tell
So-and-So about the birthdays at your house!'

These days I can understand and sympathize
with the lady I heard on the radio the other day,
who said:

I can't understand it! I was forty-
eight, and I just went into the
kitchen to make myself a cup of
coffee — and now I'm sixty-two!

27 MAY

— — —

I think this might be a good time
to recall the nun's prayer, which I
sometimes read on *Praise Be!*

Lord, thou knowest better than I
know myself
that I am growing older and will
some day be old.
Keep me from the fatal habit of
thinking I must say something on
every subject, and on every
occasion.
Release me from craving to
straighten out everybody's affairs.
Make me thoughtful, but not
moody, helpful, but not bossy.
With my vast stores of wisdom, it
seems a pity not to use it all. But
thou knowest, Lord, I want a few
friends at the end.
Keep me reasonably sweet. I do not
want to be a saint — some of them
are so hard to live with. But a sour
old person is one of the crowning
works of the Devil.
Keep my mind free from the recital
of endless details; give me wings to
get to the point.
Seal my lips on my aches and pains.
They are increasing and love of

rehearsing them is becoming
sweeter as the years go by.
I dare not ask for grace enough to
enjoy the tales of others' pains, but
help me to endure them with
patience.
I dare not ask for improved
memory but for a growing
humility, and a lessening
cocksureness when my memory
seems to clash with the memories
of others.
Teach me the glorious lesson that
occasionally I may be mistaken.
Give me the ability to see good
things in unexpected places and
talents in unexpected people.
And give me, O Lord, the grace to
tell them so.

Anon.

28 MAY

My birthday! I thought I was going to be
needed on the set for *Thora on the Broad and
Narrow* today — but they've changed the
schedule. So instead I've woken up to sunshine,
a cup of tea, and the realization of what a very
fortunate woman I am!

An old age serene and bright
And lovely as a Lapland night
Shall lead thee to thy grave.
William Wordsworth
To a young lady (1802)

29 MAY

These are the closing words of Julian's
Revelations of Divine Love:

And I saw for certain, both here
and elsewhere, that before ever he
made us, God loved us; and that his
love has never slackened, nor ever
shall. In this love all his works have
been done, and in this love he has
made everything serve us; and in
this love our life is everlasting. Our
beginning was when we were
made, but the love in which he
made us never had beginning. In it
we have our beginning.

All this we shall see in God for
ever. May Jesus grant this. Amen.
Julian of Norwich
Revelations of Divine Love
trans. Clifton Wolters

— • —

Whit Sunday

This always used to be such a big day in Manchester. I wonder if it still is? They had processions through the streets, with all the churches joining in, and the Sunday School children would be dressed in white. It was also a red-letter day for one of my aunties — because she had a very popular draper's shop where the mothers would subscribe a shilling or sixpence weekly toward the white dresses, socks, hair ribbons, underclothes and white gloves that the little girls wore. It was a lovely sight — they also wore fresh flowered crowns and carried little baskets of real flowers. It was a wonderful occasion.

Whit Sunday is the Church's birthday — the anniversary of the day when Jesus' first disciples, after he had died and risen, were filled with his Holy Spirit, and were able to carry on with the work of love he had begun.

> And it shall come to pass afterward,
> that I will pour out my spirit upon
> all flesh; and your sons and your
> daughters shall prophesy, your old
> men shall dream dreams, your
> young men shall see visions.
>
> *Joel 2:28*

31 MAY

We've said goodbye to the cottage, and packed up our things. Once more the garage at the mews is full to bursting. Never mind — who knows what tomorrow will bring?

> Man was made for joy and woe,
> And when this we rightly know
> Through the world we safely go.
>   *William Blake (1757–1827)*

JUNE

There sleeps Titania, some time
  of the night,
Lull'd in these flowers with dances
  and delight;
And there the snake throws her
  enamell'd skin,
Weed wide enough to wrap a
  fairy in.
William Shakespeare
A Midsummer-Night's Dream

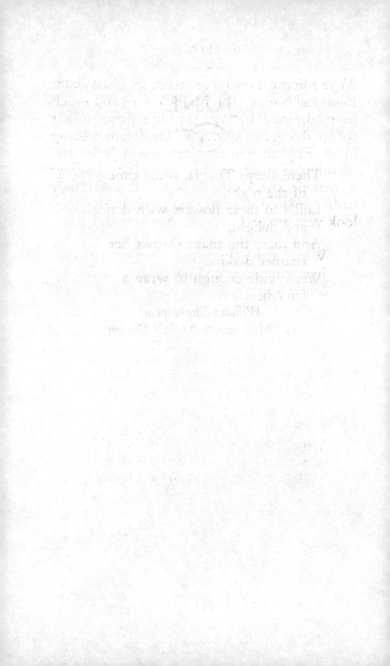

1 JUNE

We're filming a dream sequence in *Thora on the Broad and Narrow*. The Angel Voices and I each have a dream of heaven. The boys' dream is that we are flying in a spaceship. *My* dream is being in an English garden on a warm June day, surrounded by Thora Hird roses! (The designer is making them out of paper, because they hadn't ordered the real ones in time. But they look very realistic. No one but me will know.)

What's the best thing in the world?
June-rose, by May-dew impearled;
Sweet south-wind, that means no
   rain;
Truth, not cruel to a friend;
Pleasure, not in haste to end;
Beauty, not self-decked and curled
Till its pride is over-plain;
Light, that never makes you wink;
Memory, that gives no pain;
Love, when, *so,* you're loved again.
What's the best thing in the world?
— Something out of it, I think.
Elizabeth Barrett Browning (1806–61)

2 JUNE
-- --

Coronation Day

It's hard to believe that she has been our queen for over forty years now. We have known her since she was a little girl. During the Second World War King George VI and Queen Elizabeth, now the Queen Mother, their two young daughters, Elizabeth and Margaret, 'us four', the Royal Family, became *our* family.

Elizabeth was born and brought up to be a queen. I remember being so impressed by — I think it was — her first broadcast to the Commonwealth, when she was a young princess, just after the war.

> I declare before you all that my whole life, whether it be long or short, shall be devoted to your service and the service of our great Imperial family, to which we all belong.

3 JUNE
~ ~ ~

I am to be filmed at a blast-furnace today. I remember visiting one when I was a little girl, with my father, and being very frightened. But I know they'll look after us very well today.

Having had our dreams of heaven, this is supposed to be a 'Nightmare of Judgement Day' for the Angel Voices and me 'on the broad and narrow'!

Day of wrath, the years are
keeping,
When the world shall rise from
sleeping,
With a clamour of great weeping!

Earth shall fear and tremble greatly
To behold the advent stately
Of the Judge that judgeth straitly, . . .

When thy sharp wrath burns like
fire,
With the chosen of thy desire,
Call me to the crowned choir.

Prayer, like flame with ashes
blending,
From my crushed heart burns
ascending;
Have thou care for my last ending.
Algernon Charles Swinburne
(1837–1909)
from his translation of Dies Irae

4 JUNE
--

I wonder if Jan's mallard at the Mill House is missing us? 'Mother Mallard' always used to come to Jan's garden, every spring, and made her nest under the same flowering bush. But since the dreadful day when a mink — freed from a farm by so-called 'animal lovers' — savaged and killed all her ducklings, she took to choosing a different spot each year.

The year after the Great Mink Tragedy we thought she probably wouldn't come back, and there was no sign of a nest in her usual place, under the big clematis by the wall near our garden shed. Then, one day Jan was dead-heading some roses near the house, and she looked down . . . and there was 'Mother Mallard', under another clematis growing up the wall of the house, sitting proudly on fifteen eggs!

> Morning has broken
> Like the first morning,
> Blackbird has spoken
> Like the first bird.
> Praise for the singing!
> Praise for the morning!
> Praise for them, springing
> Fresh from the Word!
>   *Eleanor Farjeon (1881–1965)*

5 JUNE
-•-

Jan sometimes used to watch the mallard out of the kitchen window in the early spring, waddling round the garden with her mate, for all the world like a young couple 'viewing property'! Of course, I don't mean to imply that young couples waddle . . .

> . . . And as for the duck, I think
> God must have smiled a bit.
> Seeing those bright eyes blink on
> the day he fashioned it;
> And he's probably laughing still
> At the sound that came out of its
> bill!

6 JUNE

There's God, and Jesus, and the Holy Spirit — and when I talk to Jesus, I'm talking to God; and when I listen to God, he talks to me through the Holy Spirit . . .

> The gates of heaven are lightly
>   locked,
> We do not guard our gain,
> The heaviest hind may easily
> Come silently and suddenly
> Upon me in a lane.
>
> And any little maid that walks
> In good thoughts apart,
> May break the guard of the Three
>   Kings

And see the dear and dreadful
   things
I hid within my heart.

The meanest man in grey fields gone
Behind the set of sun,
Heareth between star and other star,
Through the door of the darkness
   fallen ajar,
The council, eldest of things that are,
The talk of the Three in One.
                    G.K. Chesterton
           The Ballad of the White Horse

7 JUNE
--

Jan and William have moved in to their new
home, and are starting a new chapter of their
life, in a new village. I've asked God to give
them every blessing.

One more step along the road I go,
One more step along the world I
   go,
From the old things to the new
Keep me travelling along with you.
And it's from the old I travel to the
   new,
Keep me travelling along with you.
                    Sydney Carter
                    One More Step

8 JUNE

But as for me, I don't know when I've seen so many faces from the past! I've been at Pinewood for the past few days, recording the studio bits for the first episode of *Thora on the Broad and Narrow*. At lunchtime I'll be having lunch in my dressing room, and there'll be a 'rat-a-tat-tat' on the door, and in will come someone — a cameraman, a wardrobe mistress or a make-up artist — saying, 'Hallo, Thora! Now when did we last work together?' It's all very loving, and I must say, I am enjoying myself!

I'll be seeing you
In all the old familiar places
That this heart of mine embraces
All day through.
Noel Coward (1899–1973)

9 JUNE

I say an extra prayer for children at school in early June, the time when they have to face their most important exams. The days are at their longest, so even after 'lights out' many a light June night is spent by anxious youngsters staring at their notebooks, trying to cram into their brains at the last minute all those dates and names, facts and figures that they'll need to know the next morning. I know how they feel — I've got so many lines to learn myself this month!

Here is a prayer we could all say.

> O God, give me your help at this
> examination time.
> Keep me from being nervous and
> keep me calm, so that I will be able
> to do my best.
> If I am not prepared, I have no
> excuse. If I am prepared, and if I
> have done my best, give me the
> calm and the freedom from nerves I
> need to do well;
> through Jesus Christ my Lord.
> Amen.

William Barclay
More Prayers for Young People

10 JUNE

For years I always said a little prayer, as I was standing in the wings of the theatre, waiting for my first entrance: 'Please God, help me to give them a good performance tonight.' Then in 1974 my brother Nev got cancer. So I always added, 'and please make Neville better'.

Then one day, it suddenly seemed to dawn on

me, that the two parts of the prayer didn't seem comparable. I thought to myself, 'Why do I say this prayer every night? The Lord has already given me my talent. I must go on and use it. My prayers should all be for Nev now.' So I said, 'Please help Neville. I'm sorry I've been asking you to help me.'

All the same, it's nice to know that the Lord is around when you are about to do something difficult or frightening, isn't it? And it's only right to thank him afterwards.

> O Lord, thou knowest how busy I must be this day; if I forget thee, do not thou forget me: for Christ's sake. Amen.
> *General Lord Astley (1579–1652)*
> *before the battle of Edgehill*

11 JUNE

In between 'takes' at Pinewood, I'm putting the finishing touches to my *Little Book of Home Truths* — a book I've written to bring together things my mother taught me, when I was growing up in Lancashire, with some of the things I've discovered for myself, about how to live a happy life. Well, I hope I haven't lived for eighty years without learning something!

One of my mother's favourite
sayings was 'Well — they're not
hurting anybody!' — a lovely
expression that condones so many
things . . .

Always make the entrances to your
home — front and back —
welcoming, by keeping them swept
clean and tidy. (Oh the *hours* I spent
as a child, blackleading the coal-
hole lid and rubbing our front door
step with a yellow rubbing stone!)

What a neighbour gets is never lost.
Thora Hird's Little Book
of Home Truths

12 JUNE

Birthday Honours

At last I can tell everyone! I've known for a few
weeks, but I couldn't even tell Jan until today.
I could hardly believe it when the letter came
— I even telephoned the number on the top, just
to make sure, because I said, 'I've already had
the OBE . . .' But it was right.

And please believe me, the best part about it
hasn't been the champagne celebrations, or the
new sign on my dressing room door — no the

best part by far has been telling Jan and Daisy and James that their Mummy and their 'Ganny' has been made a Dame!

Round the corners of the world I
   turn,
More and more about the world I
   learn.
And the new things that I see
You'll be looking at along with me.
And it's from the old I travel to the
   new,
Keep me travelling along with you.
Sydney Carter
One More Step

13 JUNE

Friends have been asking me, 'What does Scottie think about you being a Dame?'

I tell them: 'I'm still waiting to hear what Scottie thinks about my receiving the OBE — he hasn't said anything about that yet, either!' But *I* know what he thinks!

If I loved you
Words wouldn't come in an easy
   way —
Round in circles I'd go.
Oscar Hammerstein II (1895–1960)
Carousel

14 JUNE

I'd like to say something about a good friend, who is also my agent, Felix de Wolfe. We've been together now for forty-five years — on a handshake. I know a lot of artists like to have several agents, and to change them around, but I believe I would not have had nearly such a lucky and happy career as I have been blessed with, if it weren't for the good relationship I've always had with Felix.

When I first met him, I wasn't really sure, and I didn't think I wanted to be committed for seven years, which was a normal agent's and artist's contract. Over lunch I said, 'It won't be one of those seven-year things, will it?'

He said, 'I haven't decided if I'm going to take you on at all yet!'

> If our old friends should shed
> certain of their peculiarities —
> we should not like them.
> *Johann Wolfgang Von Goethe*
> *(1749–1832)*

15 JUNE

I had a very nice compliment on the radio not long ago. They were discussing Alan Bennett, that wonderfully observant writer whose plays I am always delighted to be in. I love Alan. He'll wander in to the rehearsal in his old cricket boots, looking as though he's forgotten why he's come!

On this radio programme they were saying, 'Thora Hird is an actress, like Alan Bennett with his writing, who can make you laugh and cry in the same speech.' They couldn't have said anything nicer.

I should never have tried to dust. Zulema says to me every time she comes, 'Doris. Do not attempt to dust. The dusting is my department. That's what the council pay me for. You are now a lady of leisure. Your dusting days are over.' Which would be all right provided she did dust. But Zulema doesn't dust. She half dusts. I know when a place isn't clean . . .

. . . I was glad when she'd gone, dictating. I sat for a bit looking up at me and Wilfred on the wedding photo. And I thought, 'Well, Zulema, I bet you haven't dusted the top of that.' I used to be able to reach only I can't now. So I got the buffet and climbed up. And she hadn't. Thick with dust. Home help. Home hindrance. You're better off doing it yourself. And I was

just wiping it over when, oh hell,
the flaming buffet went over.
Alan Bennett
A Cream Cracker Under the Settee

16 JUNE
--

The pier at Morecambe wasn't just a fabulous
playground for us when we were growing up
— it was much more than that. It was an
education. For instance, the John Riddings
Opera Company used to arrive every year for
a six-weeks' season on the pier. The season
included works like *Maritane, Il Trovatore, Faust,
Martha, The Bohemian Girl, Rigoletto, La Traviata,
Daughter of the Regiment* and *Lily of Killarney* . . .

All these for the pleasure and delight of the
public, and Thora and Neville Hird. I reckon
that Nev and I knew as many opera and operetta
scores — backwards — as any child in England!

A wandering minstrel I —
A thing of shreds and patches,
Of ballads, songs and snatches,
And dreamy lullaby!
W.S. Gilbert (1836–1911)
The Mikado

17 JUNE

Thought for the day:

> Life is like playing a violin in
> public and learning the instrument
> as one goes on.
>> *Samuel Butler (1612–80)*

18 JUNE

The leading lady with the John Riddings Opera Company was always called 'Miss June', a 'fine figure of a woman' as they say, and also a very fine singer. One matinee afternoon I saw Miss June coming 'up' the pier looking very smart, wearing a navy blue serge costume. The skirt reached just below her calves, the jacket was well in at the waist, and the entire cut displayed her figure to advantage. Her hat was a white panama, rather like a Breton sailor's hat, with a broad black ribbon round the crown of it.

On this particular afternoon the audience for *Faust* numbered seventeen. After the 'quarter of an hour, please', had been called, Miss June came down from her star dressing room and on to the stage. 'How's the house?' she enquired in her rich musical voice. Without waiting for an answer she proceeded to have a look for herself. She approached the swish curtain and, inserting both her thumbs in the centre part, opened them minutely and gazed with one eye through the little hole that someone had conveniently made in the Indian's canoe on the safety curtain. Then she stepped back, and declared to the empty stage as she made her exit, 'I shan't bother to change!' And she didn't!

Have you ever seen Marguerite in *Faust* played wearing a navy blue serge costume and a white Breton sailor's hat? I have!

19 JUNE

Neville's and my earlier playground, before the pier I mean, was the stage of the Royalty Theatre — during the time that my dad was Stage Director-cum-Front-of-House-Manager-cum-general-dogsbody! The theatre was next door to our home, and it was part of our home, really, because most of the time half our furniture would be being used on the stage!

Neville and I would be sent off to play on the stage whenever my mother wanted us out from under her feet. So at a very tender age Nev and I knew quite a bit about stage management — I mean we knew things like what the words brace, weight, backcloth, wings, borders, cleating and iron sheet meant. It was all part of our education.

Then to the well-trod stage anon,
If Jonson's learned sock be on,

Or sweetest Shakespeare, Fancy's
  child,
Warble his native wood-notes
  wild . . .

John Milton (1608–74)
L'Allegro

20 JUNE

After one or two 'unfortunate incidents'
involving unscheduled appearances, Nev and I
were forbidden to go on the stage during a
performance, but we were allowed on the side
during the interval, when the safety curtain was
down.

On one famous occasion there was a play
which had the same set all night, so there wasn't
the usual excitement of a scenery change in the
interval. I can only think that Nev got a bit
bored — whatever the reason, he suddenly
thought he would have a 'look through' at the
audience. Pushing his head, with his sailor cap
on, between the guide wire and the iron sheet,
he surveyed the house. He faithfully reported
anything of interest to me . . .

Then the first bell rang at the side of the stage
— the signal to start to raise the iron sheet.
Immediately the bell rang Nev started to
withdraw his head, complete with cap. As he
did so, the curtain guide wire got wedged
behind where his ear joined his head. The more

he backed, the more the wire stuck. It's all right saying that if he had gone forward again, he could have backed out sideways, but you don't think of such technicalities when you are six! He let out a piercing howl — and the entire audience looked about them in amazement. Suddenly, someone spotted the sailor cap anchored in between the side of the curtain and the wire, and shouted, 'Ee, it's little Neville Hird!'

By now Jolly Jack Tar was not only in pain but frightened to death! Dad was in the bar, but like a blue flash he reached the stage and released his son, just in time to prevent any serious damage. After that, we were restricted to *under* the stage or in the prop room!

21 JUNE
— —
Summer Solstice

If you drive from or to the West Country along the A303, you'll see Stonehenge, that ancient circle of enormous stones, more than 2,000 years old, that some people think was built by Druids for a sun-worshipping ceremony on the longest day, 21 June. You see it across the hillside, and there are always little groups of people there, standing and staring. Everyone is kept well away from the stones themselves, so they walk round and round the perimeter fence, drawn like moths to the flame of mystery.

O thou not made with hands,
Not throned above the skies,
Nor walled with shining walls,
Nor framed with stones of price,
More bright than gold or gem,
God's own Jerusalem!

F.T. Palgrave (1824–97)

22 JUNE

I don't suppose anyone is going to be exactly overjoyed to find New Age travellers or gipsies pitching camp on their doorstep. But isn't there a wee bit in all of us that understands the call of the open road? And, sometimes, don't you envy them just a tiny bit?

I remember listening to 'Romany' on the wireless, on *Children's Hour* before the war. Romany's real name was George Bramwell Evans, but his grandfather was a real gipsy — Cornelius Smith — a wild and hard-drinking man. One day he was converted to Christianity and, in the gipsy way, his whole family were converted with him! Romany's mother was Tilly Smith, Cornelius' youngest daughter, and she married a Salvation Army officer. Romany himself became a Wesleyan Methodist minister, but he never lost his ancestral gipsy love of being out and about in the natural world.

In his broadcasts Romany took his young listeners on spellbinding walks through the countryside, telling them all about the flowers, trees, birds, mammals and insects they could see. But really he never left the studio! It was all done with the magic of words, Romany's wonderful descriptive skills making you 'see' the things he was talking about. Well, you know what they say about the pictures being better on radio than television!

23 JUNE

On the radio programme *Desert Island Discs* you are invited to choose the eight records you would want to have with you on a desert island, but you can only choose one book. But it's all right, because a Gideon always gets to the island before you and leaves a Bible, and also the complete works of Shakespeare. You may be wondering 'Why Shakespeare?', but I know that if I were on a desert island today, it would be Shakespeare I would be reading myself to sleep with on this Midsummer night . . . And it would be a heart-felt prayer!

> You spotted snakes, with double
>   tongue,
> Thorny hedge-hogs, be not seen;
> Newts, and blind-worms, do no
>   wrong;

Come not near our fairy queen.

. . . Weaving spiders, come not
    here;
Hence, you long-legg'd spinners,
    hence;
Beetles black, approach not near;
Worm, nor snail, do no offence.

William Shakespeare (1564–1616)
A Midsummer-Night's Dream

24 JUNE

Midsummer Day

Another book that would be a real comfort and
delight if you *were* stranded on a desert island
would be one of the *Little Grey Rabbit* books, to
remind you of all the magic and wonder of the
English countryside.

> Squirrel and Hare were gardening
> one fine day. Squirrel was sowing
> dandelions and Hare was watering
> them. 'It's little Grey Rabbit's
> birthday on Midsummer's Day,' said
> Squirrel, as she shook the dandelion
> clocks and let the seeds fly . . . 'I
> will ask the green woodpecker or
> the goldfinch for a few feathers,
> and I'll make a little fan for her.'

'And I will make a purse for her,' said Hare . . . Hare went to the pasture for a puff-ball. He squeezed out the dust, and washed the little bag in the dew. Then he filled it with rabbit-money from the hedge, and he tied it with ribbon grasses.

Many a little animal was making a present for Grey Rabbit's birthday. Little paws were twisting rushes into baskets and carving wood-nuts and threading flowers on strings ready for Midsummer Day . . . Water-rat was down in the reed-bed among the water-lilies working by the light of the moon. Even Wise Owl had something for Grey Rabbit, and he carried his treasure under his wing when he went hunting . . .

Moldy Warp's present was the best of all. It was the song of a nightingale, in a tiny polished musical box . . .

Alison Uttley
Little Grey Rabbit's Birthday

25 JUNE

We're recording the fourth and final episode of *Thora on the Broad and Narrow*, so I'm back at Pinewood for three days. The set is rather wonderful. They've built the entire Victorian poster the programmes are based on, The Broad and Narrow Way, in three dimensions, so we can really walk along the broad path to hell, or the narrow one to heaven, and read all the Bible texts as we go!

The studio has giant outer doors, so lorries can drive in with the piano and organ and bits of scenery, and sometimes these doors will swing open during the recording, and a complete Salvation Army band and songsters come marching in and raise the roof!

> O for a thousand tongues to sing
> My dear Redeemer's praise!
> *Charles Wesley (1707–88)*

26 JUNE

My haiku for June:

Silk balloons — and me,
the tea-towel in my hand,
staring up at them.

27 JUNE

There's nothing nicer on a warm June Sunday afternoon than to take tea outside in the garden, with the scent of old-fashioned roses in the air. So it's rather a pity that I'm here at the Pinewood studio, working all day! You'll have to do the sitting in the sun for me — I know it's tough, but somebody's got to do it!

> Think of a world without any
>   flowers,
> Think of a world without any trees,
> Think of a sky without any
>   sunshine,
> Think of the air without any
>   breeze.
> We thank you, Lord, for flowers
>   and trees and sunshine,
> We thank you, Lord, and praise
>   your holy name.
>
> *Doreen Newport*
> *Come and Praise*

28 JUNE

One summer, Jan's 'Mother Mallard' had laid her eggs under a rosemary bush, and hatched out thirteen beautiful little ducklings. When they were big enough she led them all off to the lake for their first swim. They had a lovely afternoon, the dear little things bobbing about in the sunshine. But when she led them home, single file, you know, like they do, we could only see twelve little bits of fluff scrambling along behind her. (We always used to count them when they were out and about, because I don't think ducks *can* count, and we were always a bit anxious about her losing one and not noticing.)

Well, on this occasion she *had* lost one, and we all hunted high and low, searching through the reeds growing beside the lake. But we couldn't see any sign of the little lost one. After a long time searching, we were about to give up, feeling quite upset, when Jan suddenly exclaimed, 'Patch! What have you done?' (Patch, you'll remember, is half a golden retriever, the daughter of Tess — they have both appeared on *Praise Be!* — 'Family: no fee'!)

Patch was walking towards us, and dangling out of the corner of her mouth was a little, drooping, yellow head. Jan commanded 'Drop!' and Patch proudly and gently deposited the little body at her feet, the expression on her face quite clearly saying, 'I thought you'd be wanting this!'

I promise you — that little duckling was completely unharmed in the gentle retriever's 'good dog' mouth! Jan picked it up, and gave the fluffy bundle back to 'Mother Mallard'. It shook its little self and waddled off happily with its brothers and sisters.

Patch sat there with a grin on her face which said, 'I bet you thought I'd eaten it, didn't you? You dozy lot!'

29 JUNE

In 1963, in his book *Strength to Love*, Dr Martin Luther King wrote these wise words:

> The means by which we live have
> outdistanced the ends for which we
> live. Our scientific power has
> outrun our spiritual power. We have
> guided missiles and misguided men.

30 JUNE

Well, *Thora Hird's Little Book of Home Truths* is on its way to the publisher; and we've finished recording *Thora on the Broad and Narrow*, which will be going out 'on the air' next week. I wonder what people are going to make of it — it's certainly something quite different from anything I've ever done before. We shall soon see!

> What is the odds, so long as the fire
> of soul is kindled at the taper of
> conviviality, and the wing of
> friendship never moults a feather!
> *Charles Dickens (1812–70)*
> *Dick Swiveller in The Old Curiosity Shop*

JULY

In July the sun is hot.
Is it shining?
    No, it's not!

1 JULY

Very few birds sing in July — have you noticed?
It's peaceful in the early mornings because the
deafening dawn choruses have stopped! On a
summer evening you might hear a lone thrush,
or the soft chirruping of swallows and martins,
or the high-pitched radar-siren of whizzing
swifts. But our native garden birds are far too
busy stuffing food into their young ones' beaks
to sing! At noon on a baking hot July day there
is sometimes no sound at all in the garden.

> 'Tis visible silence, still as the
>   hour-glass.
> > *Dante Gabriel Rossetti (1828–82)*
> > *Silent Noon*

2 JULY

In some years, summer has hardly got started
at the beginning of July, and in other years, it's
as good as over. Whichever way it falls out,
people will talk as though such a thing has
never happened before in the whole history of
the world, and it must be the beginning of the
end!

Cold and rain and very dark. I was
sick and ill . . . William walked out
a little, I did not. We sat at the
window together. It came on a
terribly wet night. Wm. finished
'The Leech Gatherer'.

Dorothy Wordsworth
Diary, July 1802

3 JULY

You might know I receive a great number of
invitations every year to open different church
fêtes — always with the promise of a cup of tea
and a warm welcome if I do! There's nothing
like a good old-fashioned vicarage garden party
or church fête, is there? Guessing the weight of
a pig — doesn't it always have such a sad
expression?; the Mothers' Union home-made
cake stall (get there early or be killed in the
crush); tables groaning with home-made jams
and pickles; the tombola; the white elephant
stall; the coconut shy and — best of all — the tea
tent!

Yes, we'll gather at the river,
The beautiful, the beautiful, the
    river:
Gather with the saints at the river,
That flows by the throne of God.

4 JULY

American Independence Day

Jan and William will be flying both the American and the British flag at their new home today!

It's funny to think that two such typical, traditional Brits. as Scottie and myself have ended up with a half-American, half-British family. Daisy and James are both at university in California, and Jan thinks that they will choose to become American citizens. Young people interested in working in show business find America more exciting than 'the old country'. I know they will never lose their love of England, though, and will always keep returning 'home'.

> Home is the place where, when you
> have to go there,
> They have to take you in.

> I should have called it
> Something you somehow haven't to
> deserve.

> *Robert Frost (1874–1963)*

5 JULY

The first programme of *Thora on the Broad and Narrow* went out last night and was a great success. It's not for me to say whether people will like the series. It's different, I'll say that — but audiences don't always like things to be different, in my experience.

> Last Seven Words of the Church:
> We never did it that way before.

6 JULY

The inspiration behind The Broad and Narrow Way poster, and the programmes, is the preaching of Charles Haddon Spurgeon, a Victorian Baptist minister who in his day drew enormous crowds — literally in their thousands — to hear him every Sunday. The Manager of the Drury Lane Theatre said, 'I would give a large amount of money — if I could only get Spurgeon on the stage!'

> The highest glory of our holy
> religion is the cross. The history of
> grace begins earlier and goes on
> later, but in the middle point stands
> the cross. Of two eternities this is
> the hinge; of past decrees and
> future glories this is the pivot — the

vindication of divine justice, the
unexampled display of God's love, a
marvel of wisdom, a door of hope,
a source of rest . . .

Charles Haddon Spurgeon (1834–92)

7 JULY

Because I'm always reminiscing about old-fashioned customs and expressions — in my books, and on radio and television chat shows, and on *Praise Be!* — I often receive very interesting letters from people about their own memories (sometimes they're nearly as long as my books!). I was reminded by a Yorkshire lady recently about 'Spanish'. Hands up everyone who knows what 'Spanish' is . . . Right. I bet you come from Yorkshire or Lancashire, don't you?

In Yorkshire and Lancashire, 'Spanish' is what we call the black stuff in the middle of those Allsorts sweets . . . what you — if you didn't put your hand up — probably call liquorice. A favourite trick, when we were kids, was to put a couple of pieces of 'Spanish' in a bottle, fill it up with water, give it a good shake, and lo! you had a drink of Spanish Water! Great!

> Do you remember an inn,
> Miranda?
> Do you remember an inn?

And the tedding and the spreading
Of the straw for a bedding,
And the fleas that tease in the High
    Pyrenees,
And the wine that tasted of the tar?
                    Hilaire Belloc (1870–1953)

8 JULY

'You silly maggot!' That's what my mother
would have said, although I never discovered
why maggots *were* silly. And 'Dizzy lemon'.
Have you ever seen a dizzy lemon? Neither have
I, but it was another favourite expression of my
mother's.

> Mix a little foolishness with your
> serious plans:
> silliness is delightful in its place.
>   *Horace (65–8 BC)*

9 JULY

The General Synod of the Church of England
will be making *their* serious plans for the future
this week, at York: discussing the Ordination
of Women, no doubt, and the Decade of
Evangelism, and what to do with redundant
church buildings . . . It's a big business, running
a Church in the modern world.

Lord Jesus Christ, the light of the
minds, that know you,
The joy of the hearts that love you
And the strength of the wills that
serve you,
Help us so to know you that we
may truly love you,
So to love you that we may fully
serve you,
Whom to serve is perfect freedom.
after St Augustine

10 JULY

If you are making the journey by car between
Scotland and England, in either direction,
you'll be needing to stretch your legs from time
to time, won't you? Well, a place that is well
worth stopping off at so you can do that is
Hadrian's Wall. Remains of the wall and the
Roman garrisons along it are still there, and in
the nearby and aptly-named village of Wall
you'll find displays of artefacts, leather purses
and the shoes that they wore, all preserved. You
can just imagine yourself back nearly 2,000
years.

If you stand or walk on top of the wall, and
look north, you'll see a big wild landscape,
right across into the borders of Scotland. It's
good to be reminded that you are crossing from
one country to another.

A Scotchman must be a very sturdy
moralist who does not love
Scotland better than truth.
> *Dr Samuel Johnson (1709–84)*
> *Journey to the Western Islands*
> *of Scotland (1775)*

11 JULY

If you are driving down any country lane today
you'll pass hedgerows full of wild roses,
climbing higher than a double decker bus in
some places. And if, like me, you travel a lot by
train, you'll see wild foxgloves, willowgrass
and meadowsweet, turning the scrubbiest bits
of wasteland along the track into a colourful
picture.

Best of all I like to walk; time to wonder what
surprises we'll find round the next corner! I
hate to admit that because my arthritis is so bad
I'm unable to walk far. However, I thank God
that I've done my share of walking in my life
and walked miles — so I have my memories. I
shall never grumble about my painful legs
because, let's face it, some people have no
legs.

> Much struck . . . in coming from
> London by the lovely green of
> everything; certainly England gains
> more by summer or rather loses

more in winter than any country I
have seen in both seasons.

John Ruskin (1819–1900)
Letter, July 1847 (Warwickshire)

12 JULY

Someone you wouldn't necessarily associate
with comedy is the great classic writer Jane
Austen. But as you can see from the following,
she could have earned her money writing comic
scripts for television!

To Miss Cooper
Cousin,
Conscious of the Charming
Character which in every Country,
and every Clime in Christendom is
Cried, Concerning you with
Caution and Care I Commend to
your Charitable Criticism this
Clever Collection of Curious
Comments, which have been
Carefully Culled, Collected and
Classed by your Comical Cousin.
The Author

Jane Austen (1775–1817)
Letter

13 JULY

Here's someone who understood something about prayer.

> An old French peasant used to sit for hours in the church. 'What do you do all this time?' asked the priest.
>
> 'I look at him and he looks at me and we are happy,' came the reply.

14 JULY

That reminds me about 'Jim'. Jim used to go into the church every morning on his way to work. Two ticks, and bong, he was out again. One day as he was coming out he met the vicar coming in, who asked him, 'What do you do in the church, Jim? You are always in and out so quickly . . .'

'I says, "Hallo, Jesus, it's Jim," ' said Jim.

Years later Jim was very ill, in hospital. All the nurses noticed that since he had come into the ward, there seemed to be a wonderful atmosphere; all the other patients had become much more cheerful and had stopped complaining so much. One of the nurses said to Jim, 'Do you know, Jim, since you've been here, it's been ever so much nicer on the ward.'

'It isn't me,' Jim told her, 'it's my visitor.'

'But, Jim, you hardly ever get any visitors,' said the nurse in surprise.

'Yes I do,' said Jim. 'Every morning my visitor comes in, and says, "Hallo, Jim. It's Jesus." '

15 JULY

St Swithin's Day

Wouldn't you know, it's raining — and that means it'll go on raining for the next forty days, according to the legend. After three years of drought, the underground streams and rivers in the South of England need it, and it looks as though this is going to be one of the wettest years on record.

> St Swithun's Day, if thou dost rain,
> For forty days it will remain:
> St Swithun's Day, if thou be fair,
> For forty days 'twill rain na mair.

16 JULY

As well as vicarage garden parties and church fêtes, this is the time of year when many people will be opening their garden gates to the public, and charging 50p admittance! Really, it's well worth going to these 'garden openings'. And you could hardly call them amateur, most of them. More and more people are becoming expert at making their gardens beautiful, even if they've got little more than a back yard. In fact, sometimes it's the smaller gardens that are most worthwhile visiting, to see the ingenious way they have been designed. And of course, the money raised all goes to a good cause. Whatever the size, they will all be praying the weather won't let them down.

It's a lovely day tomorrow!
Tomorrow is a lovely day!
Come and feast your fair blue eyes
On tomorrow's fair blue skies . . .

17 JULY
—-—

July Haiku
Glow-worms in the night —
How pretty. But well for them
Children are in bed!

Hey! Isn't it about time you had a go at one of these?

18 JULY

After a 'conversion' experience, Charles Haddon Spurgeon travelled from his village in Cambridgeshire to London, where — at age *seventeen* — he became minister of a small Baptist church. He and his sermons were so popular that within ten years he had built the largest chapel in Britain, able to hold 6,000 people, and always full. As well as being a wonderful preacher, he would urge his congregation to be regular with their private prayer. His own private prayers were rather arresting, too.

> Lord, accept me; I here present
> myself, praying to live only for
> thee.
> Let me be as the bullock which
> stands between the plough and the
> altar, to work, or to be sacrificed;
> and let my motto be, 'Ready for
> either'.
> *Charles Haddon Spurgeon (1834–92)*

19 JULY

There are millions and millions of poppies in the fields this year — more than I can ever remember. Scottie and I drove past some fields the other day and I thought we were looking

at the Red Sea! They seem to grow especially
well in the oilseed rape fields, after the yellow
has faded.

> The sleep-flower sways in the
> wheat its head,
> Heavy with dreams, as that with
> bread:
> The goodly grain and the sun-
> flushed sleeper
> The reaper reaps, and Time the
> reaper.
>
> *Francis Thompson*
> *The Poppy*

20 JULY

Farms don't look the same any more. Once
every farmer in Kent and Worcestershire would
be growing hops, and at this time of year the
green vines would be twisting up the giant
poles. Now you are as likely to find acres of
Christmas trees, or even a vineyard, as a hop
garden in Kent. And every year all over the
country there seems to be more and more and
bigger and bigger fields of bright yellow
oilseed rape, and blue flax, where once there
would have been hay, corn, wheat and barley
fields, surrounded by hedges. I suppose they
know what they're doing.

Jesus must have been looking across at the

fields and farms on the hills of Galilee when the crowds followed him down to the beach, and he got into a little boat and put out to sea a little to talk to them.

> Behold, there went out a sower to sow:
> And it came to pass, as he sowed, some fell by the way side, and the fowls of the air came and devoured it up.
> And some fell on stony ground, where it had not much earth; and immediately it sprang up, because it had no depth of earth:
> But when the sun was up, it was scorched; and because it had no root, it withered away.
> And some fell among thorns, and the thorns grew up, and choked it, and it yielded no fruit.
> And other fell on good ground, and did yield fruit that sprang up and increased; and brought forth, some thirty, and some sixty, and some an hundred.
>
> *Mark 4:3–8*

21 JULY

One of the saddest things is when you have a much-loved family dog or cat, and it becomes so ill, or has so much pain, you know that it's kindest to have it put to sleep. Like our dear little Lucy a few years ago, God rest her. It's such a hard thing to have to do. A neighbour of a friend of ours wrote this touching poem after his dog, Magnum, a Doberman Pinscher who had become crippled with arthritis, was put out of his pain this summer.

> I took my dog to see the vet the
> other day and watched
> him limp along the street and
> through the door to wait his turn.
> He lay there as we talked and
> shook our heads, not moving when
> we killed his pain, but sighed and
> fell into a breathless sleep.
>
> But now, perhaps, he woke and
> stirred, shook off my tears
> and stretched new limbs to race
> into the welcome night —
> around the sky, across the stars,
> towards the dawn.
> And when at last the boatman
> answered to his bark,
> my bronze-black dog stood in the
> bow, head raised to scent

the haunted, pastoral fragrance of
Elysium.

A.W. Drummond
A Consoling Phantasy

22 JULY
- -
St Mary Magdalene

In his loving friendship with Mary Magdalene,
Jesus demonstrated the courtesy and kindness
of God to us all.

There's a wideness in God's mercy
Like the wideness of the sea;
There's a kindness in his justice
Which is more than liberty.

There is no place where earth's
sorrows
Are more felt than up in heaven;
There is no place where earth's
failings
Have such kindly judgement given.

F.W. Faber (1814–63)

23 JULY
- -

I remember going on a picnic with my school
nature-study class, and visiting a tiny village
shop to buy presents to take back to my family

with the sixpence I had been given to spend.

It was easy to decide on my dad's gift — five Woodbines in a little paper packet, *twopence!* My present to my mother was a bit more difficult and a great deal of lip chewing took place before I took the plunge. On the short wooden counter in the village shop, along with other tempting goodies, was a box of necklaces made of stamped white celluloid, and from each one hung a pendant. It was the choice of the pendant I found so difficult. At long last — and I swear no customer buying diamonds in Asprey's or Cartier's chose with greater care — I decided on a small oval one with a little Cupid painted on it. The only drawback about the Cupid was that one of its eyebrows was very high up and the other one very low down, giving it a rather quizzical look. However, it was the best of the bunch, so I bought it — *threepence!* I bought Nev my brother a slate pencil, halfpenny, and myself ten aniseed balls . . . then I was spent up.

On the Friday after my gifts had been given and received with great pleasure, my parents were invited out to dinner by some friends. When my mother was all dressed up and ready to go, she came upstairs to kiss us goodnight and God bless. When she leaned over to kiss me as I lay in bed, something lightly tickled my chin — it was the pendant! My present, bought with my threepence! She was wearing it! I remember thinking how *nice* she looked in her lovely brown crêpe de chine dress and her tiny pearl earrings. 'Do you think everybody will like it?' I enquired — meaning the pendant.

'Like it? I'm sure everyone will envy me,' she assured me. What a brave woman — a lovely dress and a threepenny pendant! I don't wonder Cupid looked worried!

24 JULY

I still enjoy bargain hunting, and I sometimes go with Scottie and his sister, Rita, to car boot sales. I now have in my possession a beautiful little pottery jug from one such boot sale the summer before last. I'll tell you what happened.

The man selling it had a number of little pottery things, but I noticed the jug at once, and picked it up to look at it. 'It's Thora, isn't it' he said.

I said, 'Yes, it is, and I was admiring this little jug. How much do you want for it?'

'You can have it,' he said at once.

'No, I don't want to have it — I want to *buy* it,' I said.

He said, 'I always watch you on *Praise Be!* My wife and I always watched you together. But I've lost her. She died a few weeks ago, and I'm that unhappy. Please have it.'

'Oh I am sorry,' I said. 'You feel as if you've got a big brick in your heart, don't you? And it feels as though it will never go away?'

'Oh yes,' he said. 'It does. I'll never get over it.'

'God gives you that brick,' I said, 'because of how much you loved your wife. When there's a lot of love, you can't just feel nothing when your partner dies. But the brick will gradually melt away. You won't even notice at first, but one day you'll realize that it's got a bit less. You'll still have all your loving memories — but the brick will go.'

Anyway, he insisted that I take the jug, and now I keep yellow flowers in it. And when I look at it I say a little prayer to Him upstairs — not that he needs reminding.

25 JULY

— —

I'm *Thora on the Broad and Narrow* for the last time tonight. The Angel Voices are singing a song I remember so well from Sunday School.

> Jesus bids us shine
> With a pure, clear light,
> Like a little candle,
> Burning in the night.
> In this world of darkness
> So let us shine,
> You in your small corner
> And I in mine.
> *Susan Warner (1819–85)*

—•—

You may have noticed that I don't exactly have a lot of lines to learn for my part in *Last of the Summer Wine* — none of us women usually do. Even for the men, it's written more like a strip cartoon than a play. But I do enjoy the bits of comic 'business' it involves. It gives me a chance to use some of my old 'stage craft'.

For instance, when the women all come to my — I mean Edie's — house for coffee and gossip, what makes the scene funny is if we all lift our teacups at exactly the same second. It's funny when that happens in life, if you suddenly notice you're all lifting your cups at the same instant. And I enjoy my bits of fussing with the newspaper, so that anywhere my husband, Wesley, starts to put his hands, feet or head, I've whipped in a bit of newspaper under him. And what makes that funnier is if I can do it without even looking at him.

> I don't mind living in a man's world, as long as I can be a woman in it.
>
> *Marilyn Monroe*

27 JULY

—•—

My real-life husband, Scottie, needs no such administrations . . . well, sometimes people do ask!

When we met, Scottie was a professional drummer in a top-class band, and a first-rate musician. The war interrupted his career, when he went to serve with the RAF, while I was just beginning to make my name as an actress. If Scottie had gone back to being a full-time professional musician and pursued his own career when he was demobbed, I've no doubt he would have been a great success. I've also no doubt that we wouldn't still be together. One artist and one marriage needs two people working full-time — at both.

Without Scottie as my partner, I don't know what sort of career I would have had. Like my dad, he has never been one to say, 'Oh, you were good!' — but I do know that I would have missed the best support that anyone could ever ask for — as well as the severest bloomin' critic!

> It was also ordained for the mutual
> society, help, and comfort that the
> one ought to have of the other,
> both in prosperity and adversity.
> *Scottish Prayer Book (1929)*
> *Solemnization of Matrimony*

28 JULY
— —

The other thing that is probably quite well known about 'my feller' by now, I mean by more than just the friends who visit us, is that

he is a splendiferous cook — I say that in all
sincerity. There's something fundamentally
good and important about sharing delicious
meals with someone you love. If someone slams
a bit of heated-up pizza on an unwarmed plate
and calls it lunch, they are missing such a lot.
To me, the delicious smell of freshly cooked
vegetables that emanates from our kitchen
every lunchtime is forever associated with love
and happiness and laughter and friends.

> For food and drink and happy days,
> Accept our gratitude and praise;
> In serving others, Lord, may we
> Repay in part our debt to thee.

29 JULY
St Martha

Martha may have got herself into too much of
a fuss about preparing meals for her guests, but
I think there is no doubt that Jesus loved her
very dearly.

> Then Martha, as soon as she heard
> that Jesus was coming, went and
> met him: but Mary sat still in the
> house.
> Then said Martha unto Jesus, 'Lord,
> if thou hadst been here, my brother
> had not died.

But I know, that even now,
whatsoever thou wilt ask of God,
God will give it thee.'
Jesus saith unto her, 'Thy brother
shall rise again.'
Martha saith unto him, 'I know
that he shall rise again in the
resurrection at the last day.'
Jesus said unto her, 'I am the
resurrection, and the life: he that
believeth in me, though he were
dead, yet shall he live:
And whosoever liveth and believeth
in me shall never die. Believest thou
this?'

John 11:20–26

30 JULY
−−

I appeared in an opera once . . . I thought that might impress you! I've mentioned the John Riddings Opera Company — but I don't think I told you that I actually appeared in *The Bohemian Girl.*

I didn't have to sing! I was the child carried off over the rocks by Devilshoof, the gipsy king. There knelt my heart-broken father (John Riddings himself, no less) and my stage mother, and all the servants — eyes closed (but of course! otherwise they would have seen Devilshoof carrying me off across the rocks behind them!), hands together in prayer, singing softly.

As the gipsy king and I approached our exit, I can vividly remember thinking, 'Well, I haven't done much!' So, before we disappeared off-stage, I assumed a heart-broken voice, and stretching my arms towards the praying family I wailed, 'Daddy! Daddy!' Poor Devilshoof nearly dropped me on the prop rocks! Oh dear, I thought everyone would be so pleased, but I didn't realize that I'd called out so loudly that, even allowing for stage licence, 'Daddy and Mummy' must have appeared stone deaf not to have heard me!

But they kept me on, and my salary was a bottle of lime juice and soda per performance.

> He who turns his nose up at his work, quarrels with his bread and butter.
> *Charles Haddon Spurgeon*

31 JULY

I stood on Morecambe Promenade on 31 July 1933 — sixty years ago today — watching the Central Pier Pavilion burn down. The small dome on the left crumbled first, and disappeared. The gallant centre dome went on standing proud and magnificent, trying to defy the flames as they curled round its base, but the arms of fire reached greedily upwards and embraced it in a cruel bright red cloak. It was soon entirely ablaze and as the massive flames reached to the sky it looked as though it was frantically trying to cling or clutch to something. With a heart-breaking wail it collapsed . . .

So many memories. I ached with sadness as I wondered how much longer my vestal virgins could hold the boxes up. Of course, they had never held up the boxes really, had they? I can remember thinking, 'I bet they are valiantly trying to hold them up now!'

The papers reported that it was Morecambe's biggest fire to date. How like the Central Pier! Nothing but the best. 'Everyone on stage for the finale, please!'

It was there; it was there no longer. All in ninety minutes. A sad day.

> Dearest Lord, teach me to be generous;
> Teach me to serve thee as thou deservest;
> To give and not to count the cost,
> To fight and not to heed the wounds,
> To toil and not to seek for rest,
> To labour and not to seek reward,
> Save that of knowing that I do thy will.
> *St Ignatius of Loyola (1491–1556)*

AUGUST

August for the people and their
   favourite islands
Daily the steamers sidle up to meet
The effusive welcome of the pier.
   W.H. Auden (1907–73)

1 AUGUST

On *Summer Praise,* August is 'for the people and their favourite *hymns*'! Tonight it was a voyage — 'doon the watter' — from Glasgow. The steamer received an 'effusive welcome of the pier' from local congregations and choirs at various Clyde-side towns and villages along the lovely Firth. One such place was Innellan, where a Scottish poet and minister, George Matheson, wrote one of the most profound and moving hymns in the English language: 'O Love that wilt not let me go'.

> O Love that wilt not let me go,
> I rest my weary soul in thee:
> I give thee back the life I owe,
> That in thine ocean depths its flow
> May richer, fuller be.
> *Revd George Matheson (1842–1906)*
> *Sacred Songs*

2 AUGUST

I thought I hadn't seen little Lena Zavaroni on television for a long time — do you remember her when she won *Opportunity Knocks* and became a child star? She looked like — and was — a little girl then, but she had a big voice. When she was interviewed on last night's *Summer Praise,* she said that the reason she had been out of the public eye for so long was because she's had that terrible anorexia thing, and had been close to death.

Everyone dreams of success — but too much too soon can cause as much stress as failure, particularly if it comes when you are still very young and inexperienced, as she was, poor little mite. She's a young woman now, still frail-looking, but she said on the programme that she keeps going because she clings on to the thought that 'hope' is a word . . .

I shall remember her in my prayers tonight.

O Joy that seekest me through
     pain,
I cannot close my heart to thee:
I trace the rainbow through the
     rain,
And feel the promise is not vain
That morn shall tearless be.
Revd George Matheson (1842–1906)
Sacred Songs

3 AUGUST

There's a brownish look to fields and gardens in August. It's still summer, but without any freshness to it. The best place to be is beside the sea — even if you can't always depend on the sunshine . . .

Tintagel. Black cliffs and caves and
storm and wind, but I weather it
out and take my ten-miles-a-day
walks in my weather-proofs.

Alfred, Lord Tennyson
1860 (Cornwall)

4 AUGUST

Her Majesty Queen Elizabeth, the Queen
Mother, is ninety-three today. In celebration
there will be peals rung from church towers all
across Britain. And when the Guards return to
their barracks after 'Changing the Guard', they
will pause outside Clarence House to play
'Happy Birthday To You' on fife and drum to
give her a happy start to her day. By the time her
daughters arrive for a family birthday lunch, so
many flowers will be being handed in at the gates
by well-wishers, she'll need a fork-lift truck to
transport them all! What a greatly loved person
she is, and how lucky we are to have her!

You shall go out with joy
and be led forth with peace,
and the mountains and the hills
shall break forth before you.
There will be shouts of joy —
and the trees of the field shall clap
their hands
and you'll go out with joy.

S. Dauermann

5 AUGUST

The roses are fading, leaves hang tired and heavy on the trees, and everything seems torpid; but in August the world is made beautiful by butterflies! Chrysalises which have lain dormant all winter hatch out, and butterflies dance around the sedum and buddleia flowers, or sunbathe on warm walls and paths, fanning their wings. They must lay their eggs soon for the next generation.

Don't ask me what this next bit means — I've just found it in the *Dictionary of Quotations* and liked it!

> I do not know whether I was then
> a man dreaming I was a butterfly,
> or whether I am now a butterfly,
> dreaming I am a man.
> *Chuang Tse (4th–3rd century BC)*
> *trans. H.A. Giles*

6 AUGUST

The Transfiguration

I always think this is the most mysterious episode in the whole of the gospels. Was it a dream or a vision — or did it really happen?

Jesus took Peter and John and James, and went up into a mountain to pray.

And as he prayed, the fashion of his countenance was altered, and his raiment was white and glistening.

And, behold, there talked with him two men, which were Moses and Elias:

Who appeared in glory, and spake of his decease, which he should accomplish at Jerusalem.

But Peter and they that were with him were heavy with sleep: and when they were awake, they saw his glory, and the two men that stood with him.

Luke 9:28–32

7 AUGUST

In any seaside town you'll find a large proportion of its residents are elderly people, bustling all over town. Even the more fragile can be seen walking purposively down the Prom. on sticks and walking frames, or 'still rolling along with one wheel on my waggon' in wheel-chairs and invalid cars.

The sticker, which I saw in the back of an old gentleman's Mini once, is true for anyone over the 'three score years and ten' I reckon:

Old age ain't for sissies!

8 AUGUST

Doris, the old lady I played in Alan Bennett's play *A Cream Cracker under the Settee*, had one dread — and that was that she would be sent to live in Stafford House, a council old people's home.

> When people were clean and the streets were clean and it was all clean and you could walk down the street and folks smiled and passed the time of day, I'd leave the door on the latch and go on to the end for some toffee, and when I came back Dad was home and the cloth was on and the plates out and we'd have our tea. Then we'd side the pots and I'd wash up while he read the paper and we'd eat the toffees and listen to the wireless all them years ago when we were first married and I was having the baby.
>
> Doris and Wilfred. They don't get called Doris now. They don't get called Wilfred. Museum names like that. That's what they're all called in Stafford House. Alice and Doris. Mabel and Gladys. Antiques.

Keep them under lock and key.
'What's your name? Doris? Right.
Pack your case. You belong in
Stafford House.'
A home. Not me. No fear.

Alan Bennett
A Cream Cracker Under the Settee

9 AUGUST

In many seaside resorts the growing elderly
population get themselves organized — Senior
Citizens' Rights groups, Drop-in Centres,
Help the Aged and Citizens' Advice Bureaux.
As often as not they are manned by volunteers
who are elderly and retired themselves, all
giving advice and help to people who've come
unstuck in some way — with money problems,
or are lonely, or who feel they are being
exploited — an all too common experience in
some of the private so-called 'homes'. It isn't
home for a frail old person if there's no warmth
or kindness or companionship, or anyone with
time and patience to listen to their worries.

Clemency Greatorex from Goudhurst is one
of the people who has sent me beautiful prayers
over the years on *Praise Be!* Here is one for the
semi-invalid.

From the fear of getting worse
Good Lord, deliver us;

From self-pity and the temptation
to play for sympathy
    Good Lord, deliver us;
From the fear that others may think
we are making a fuss
    Good Lord, deliver us;
From self-conscious pride in
fighting bravely against illness
    Good Lord, deliver us;
From refusal to accept help kindly
offered
    Good Lord, deliver us.
When we are enclosed in trouble,
and cannot look outwards
    Dear Lord, be with us.

Amen
Clemency Greatorix

10 AUGUST
—

Carnival Week at Morecambe when I was a
child used to be a high point in our year.
Everyone went about dressed in Carnival
costumes — rock pink and pale blue —
enthusiastically 'run up' in pink and blue sateen,
which was about 9½d a yard; throwing
streamers and confetti at each other and
blowing 'tommy talkers'. We always had a sack
of confetti at Number 6 Cheapside, so that we
could fill and refill a large bag to take with us
as we went out! None of your small twopenny
packets — a sack!

A Carnival song was composed each year and everyone sang it lustily. One I can remember went something like this:

> It's carnival time once more, it's
>   carnival time once more.
> Young and old come from near and
>   from far
> To join in the fun and say 'Well,
>   here we are!
> — Hey, Willie, why, lad it's you — I
>   thought I'd seen you before!'
> Cheerio! Toodle-oo! It's a right
>   champion do
> It's carnival time once more!

Anon.
Morecambe Carnival song

11 AUGUST

Another wonder of the Morecambe Carnival were the illuminations! The flowerbeds in the Promenade gardens were a mass of twinkling lights. This magical effect was achieved by placing thousands of night lights in little coloured glass containers. They were replaced and lit each evening by hordes of volunteers armed with tapers and matches. How they used to pray for a calm evening!

Isn't it amazing how people always state the obvious? As you walked along the Prom. you would hear this remark dozens of times: 'Oh look — there's one gone out!' or 'Oh look! there's one there not in!' Never mind all the thousands of others that *were* there, twinkling away — it was the ones that had given up the ghost that were noticed the most!

I somehow don't think they'd find it very easy today to find so many willing volunteers to give up their time to light candles just for the pleasure of others.

> God does not want us to do
> extraordinary things; he wants us to
> do ordinary things extraordinarily
> well.
> *Bishop Charles Gore (1853–1932)*

12 AUGUST

Have you ever noticed that if you see a robin in August, it'll be looking rather scruffy? Their new red feathers are only just beginning to grow on their breasts, and red and brown feathers stick out all over the place. They look as though they've just got out of bed and need a good comb!

> We must all obey the great law of
> change. It is the most powerful law
> of nature.
> *Edmund Burke (1729–97)*

13 AUGUST

— —

I read in my paper that 'the glorious twelfth' of August has turned out not to be very glorious this year — at any rate, not from the point of view of those sportsmen who like to go out on the moors and shoot grouse. There weren't enough grouse for them to shoot, so it was cancelled. No, I'm not losing too much sleep over it.

> Entirely calm and clear morning.
> The mist from the river at rest
> among the trees, with rosy light on
> its folds of blue; and I, for the first
> time these ten years, happy.
>
> *John Ruskin*
> *13 August 1872 (Berkshire)*

14 AUGUST

— —

The harvest is under way, and it's beautiful to walk across stubble fields — startling a few hares and field mice!

In St Matthew's gospel there's the story about a farmer who sowed good seed. But in the night an enemy came, and the next day the land was full of thistles, and he said, 'An enemy hath done this!' (I often used to think 'an enemy

213

hath done this' when I looked at the weeds that came up overnight in our garden!)

In the parable, the farmer doesn't dig out all the thistles, in case it hurts the wheat. He lets the thistles and the wheat grow together, and tells his men that at harvest time they must sort them all out, and burn the thistles and store the wheat safely in the barn.

It's good to know that even when God doesn't remove the thistles growing up around us — like the thistles of sadness, loneliness, illness and pain — the wheat is still growing.

> Let both grow together until the
> harvest.
> *Matthew 13:30*

15 AUGUST
--

Another royal birthday today — the Princess Royal. Among all the many good things she does, Princess Anne works especially hard in her role as President of the Save the Children charity.

Save the Children have managed, almost miraculously, to airlift some injured children out of Bosnia this week, and we're all praying for the success of 'Operation Irma'. Irma is a little girl whose mother was killed by a mortar bomb, and Irma herself is terribly badly injured and will need to be treated in Great Ormond

Street Children's Hospital.

You know the old Chinese proverb: 'Don't curse the darkness — light a candle'? Well now, in the darkness and confusion of Sarajevo, someone *has* lit a candle. A medical team has flown out from Scotland, and at least some of the many hundreds of dangerously ill children like Irma will be brought safely back here to receive treatment. Others will follow. It's a little less dark out there.

I don't think Her Royal Highness would ask for a better birthday present.

> A man can do only what he can do. But if he does that each day he can sleep at night and do it again the next day.
> *Albert Schweitzer (1875–1965)*

16 AUGUST

On 16 August 1970 Scottie and I went to the North, to Blackpool on business. We also visited my brother Nev and his wife Lily in Morecambe, to help celebrate Nev's birthday. (It's not only the Royal Family who have birthdays in August to celebrate, you know . . . the Hirds do, too!)

'Admiral' Hird took us on 'a Mystery Tour — back for tea'. It was a journey of many happy memories through the Lancashire countryside and villages I knew so well. But as we approached the outskirts of Morecambe Nev warned me, 'Prepare yourself for a bit of a shock, our kid.'

'Oh, it's all right!' I said, 'I mean — I know it's not there, is it? I mean, Cheapside, the Royalty — it's all *gone*, hasn't it?'

'Yes,' Nev said, looking straight ahead as he drove along. 'It's all gone.'

By the time we arrived at Cheapside, Neville had assumed the guise of a guide on a conducted tour: 'And here we have — Cheapside!' he announced. But just a minute! It *couldn't* be Cheapside. Cheapside was never a *little* street — was it? It all looked so little now. If you knock houses down to ground level and clear the rubble away, it should all look so much *bigger*, shouldn't it? But here even the roadway — the part that had escaped the bulldozers — was only little.

As I looked at the rubble, I wondered what would be built on the little patch where Number 6 had stood. I hoped it would contain as much happiness and love as our house did. I hoped that whoever lived or worked there would be as gay and have as big a sense of humour as the Hirds had had.

'Come on, love,' said Scottie.

'Yes — let's go,' said Nev.

17 AUGUST

I've been back to Morecambe many times over the years, and sometimes the television cameras have come with me — once for a special *Songs of Praise* from Morecambe. That was great! Everytime we started filming the introduction, another old friend would come over, saying, 'Ee! *Thora*? Is it really you?' I'd have a lovely chat, but then we'd have to start the filming all over again!

The hymn-singing was accompanied by the local Salvation Army band, with their conductor. And there was also a conductor for us, in the congregation, so there were two conductors, do you follow? One of the hymns we sang was one of my great favourites, because it reminds me of my uncles, who were Morecambe fishermen: 'Will your anchor hold?'

All right so far. The Salvation Army band leader raised his baton, our conductor raised his baton, and then the band was away like an express train: 'Terra-rum-pum-pum-terra-rum-pum-pum!' — getting to the end of the first verse and chorus in about twenty seconds flat! 'Our' conductor, his baton still poised gracefully in the air, turned very slowly round and just *looked*. The Salvation Army band conductor turned round too, still conducting, and pretending to look very surprised that we hadn't started singing yet! It was quite a comedy routine, part of a very loving evening of laughter and hymn-singing.

> Will your anchor hold in the
> storms of life
> When the clouds unfold their wings
> of strife?
> When the strong tides lift, and the
> cables strain,
> Will your anchor drift, or firm
> remain?
>> *Priscilla Jane Owens (1829–99)*

18 AUGUST
— —

When you are by the sea, with its changing tides, it's hard to stop your mind turning to thoughts about time and eternity, and to wonder if you've spent your own time as well as you might. Here is a prayer about time.

> **Time**
> Lord, help us to teach children to
> use it joyfully, and teenagers to use
> it sensibly.
> Please help grown-ups never to be
> harassed by the lack of it,
> and the old to live peacefully in the
> superfluity of it.
>> *Clemency Greatorix (1993)*

19 AUGUST

The journalist and broadcaster Stewart Lamont is also a Church of Scotland minister. During a time when he was working full-time in religious broadcasting he didn't have his own church, but he was frequently invited to preach in other ministers' pulpits.

On one such occasion the invitation had come from a minister in his home town. Stewart arrived in very good time, but nobody was there to greet him, and although he found someone to show him where he could change into his gown, he felt that they seemed quite surprised to see him. However, he got himself ready, and then looked round the robing room, where there were photographs on the walls. To his amazement the photograph of the minister on the wall wasn't a picture of the man he knew, who had invited him to preach.

Light dawned — he was in the wrong church! He looked at his watch — seconds to go until the service was due to begin! He picked up his bags and sped down the aisle, fully gowned, past the minister who was greeting his flock at the door. He must have been amazed to see a strange minister, fully gowned, fleeing from his church. 'Good morning, Minister. Wrong church!' panted our hero, as he ran off down the road to the church next-door, where he was meant to be!

Climb every mountain
Ford every stream
Follow every highway
'Til you find your dream!

> Oscar Hammerstein II
> *The Sound of Music*

20 AUGUST

Here is the prayer of another Church of Scotland minister, one of William Barclay's evening prayers for the Plain Man.

Eternal and ever blessed God, help
us this night to lay ourselves down
in peace.
Give us that peace of mind, which
comes from casting all our burdens
upon thee, and from leaving
ourselves and our loved ones
entirely to thy care.
Give us that peace which comes
from being in perfect personal
relationships with our fellows, with
no misunderstandings between us
and them, and with no bitterness to
anyone.
Give us the peace of sins forgiven,
which comes from the certainty that,
through Jesus Christ, there is no
barrier between ourselves and thee.

And, above all, give us the peace of
thy presence, and the certainty that
in light and dark thou wilt never
leave us, nor forsake us, and that
thou wilt never let us go.
Amen.

21 AUGUST
--

I do hope you've come across Sister Wendy
Beckett, and her wonderful ten-minute
programmes about art. Have you? Sister Wendy
has lived alone for the past twenty years in a
little caravan in East Anglia, praying for seven
hours a day, working for two hours, and much
of the rest of her time has been spent in
contemplating postcard reproductions of great
works of art. This year, for the first time in
twenty years, she has emerged from her
caravan, and a television crew has accompanied
her to visit the originals of all the paintings she
has grown to love from the postcards. She
shares her enthusiasm and knowledge with us
all in such a wonderful way, it's impossible not
to be bowled over by her. Then she goes back
to her caravan.

When Sister Wendy is asked *why* she has
chosen to live such a solitary life, she says that
she knows that God created us to live in
community with one another, but every now

and then someone comes along who just can't manage relationships with other people. Then God says, 'Well, I've got a complete dud here! I'd better find her a caravan to live in, out of everybody's way!'

God tempers the wind to the shorn lamb.

Laurence Sterne (1713–68)

22 AUGUST

Anyone living in a seaside town has to say goodbye to their friends and neighbours for August, because the local population changes from 2,000 to 20,000 overnight, so you know you might not see them in the crowd!

Many more people go abroad for their summer holidays than did when I was growing up, but the British family holiday at the seaside still goes on — buckets and spades, donkey rides, sticks of rock, the lot! And where would the theatrical profession be without it? The shows at the end of the pier, the brass bands, the illuminations, and all the singers and comics who got their start by becoming Redcoats at the seaside holiday camps — all belong to the traditional family holiday.

In more and more places you may also find the churches have laid on an open-air hymn-sing — whether the BBC are there to record it

or not! Have you ever praised the Lord in a
steady drizzle or a force nine gale? At the seaside
the good old British public button up their
mackintoshes, up go the umbrellas, and they
will keep right on singing!

> Summer suns are glowing
> Over land and sea;
> Happy light is flowing,
> Bountiful and free.
> Everything rejoices
> In the mellow rays;
> All earth's thousand voices
> Swell the psalm of praise.
> *William Walsham How (1823–97)*

23 AUGUST

It isn't *always* raining! And the long hot days of
August can be quite a trial for anyone who isn't
well. The words of this next hymn, based on
words from St Matthew's gospel, are like a
prayer for anyone feeling a bit 'under par'.

> At even, ere the sun was set,
> The sick, O Lord, around thee lay;
> O in what divers pains they met!
> O with what joy they went away!
>
> O Saviour Christ, our woes dispel;
> For some are sick, and some are sad,

And some have never loved thee well,
And some have lost the love they had;

And some have found the world is
  vain,
Yet from the world they break not
  free;
And some have friends who give
  them pain,
Yet have not sought a friend in thee;

And none, O Lord, have perfect rest,
For none are wholly free from sin;
And they who fain would serve thee
  best
Are conscious most of wrong within.

Thy touch has still its ancient power;
No word from thee can fruitless fall:
Hear, in this solemn evening hour,
And in thy mercy heal us all.

H. Twells (1823–1900)

24 AUGUST

North of the border, August means the start of the Edinburgh Festival. Someone worked out that it would take one year, eleven months, nine days, two hours and twenty-four minutes to see every 'fringe' show at this year's Festival . . . There's something for everyone this year — from the new sensation, *Mr Lifto*, to four different productions of *Much Ado About Nothing!*

A victory is twice itself when the achiever brings home full numbers.
William Shakespeare
Much Ado About Nothing

25 AUGUST

The only trouble with 'the fringe' of the Edinburgh Festival is, well, I don't know where else you'll have to stand for so long in so many queues! You even have to queue to get into the place . . . where you queue. And then, after you've queued to get into the queue for tickets, you have to queue somewhere else to get into the show itself. And you can't help getting the uneasy feeling that you're in the wrong queue, because all the time you are queueing for one thing, people are pressing leaflets and information into your hands that tell you that something else — a show you simply must not miss — is just about to start somewhere else!

But if you are the sort of person who always wonders if they aren't spending their whole life in the wrong queue, don't worry. In the end, you discover it doesn't really matter. Everything is grist to the mill. The queueing beforehand, making friends with the complete strangers in front and behind you, the coffee and conversation, even falling asleep in an exhausted heap on the pavement afterwards are the important times — not the shows themselves. It won't matter even if you find you've queued for all four versions of *Much Ado About Nothing* and missed out on *Mr Lifto* altogether . . .

> Then sigh not so,
> But let them go,
> And be you blithe and bonny,
> Converting all your sounds of woe
> Into Hey nonny, nonny.
> *William Shakespeare*
> *Much Ado About Nothing*

26 AUGUST

An August Haiku
Big horse in the shade
Of the spreading chestnut tree
flicking away flies.

27 AUGUST

Tired gardens start to come to life again towards the end of August with second flowerings in the herbaceous border of roses, catmint and ladies' mantle. Pots of morning glory produce their wonderful blue flowers, new ones every day, that fade and die by evening, to be replaced by more next morning. Honeysuckle is in its glory, and clematis is growing up through dull leafy shrubs, making them colourful with deep red flowers.

> A garden is a lovesome thing, God
>   wot!
> Rose plot,
> Fringed pool,
> Ferned grot —
> The veriest school
> Of peace; and yet the fool
> Contends that God is not —
> Not God! in gardens! when the eve is
>   cool?
> Nay, but I have a sign:
> 'Tis very sure God walks in mine.
>   *T.E. Brown (1830–97)*

28 AUGUST

On 28 August 1906, the Scottish poet and minister, George Matheson, died. There is an old story that he wrote the words of his great hymn 'O Love that wilt not let me go' in a mood of great sadness after the girl that he loved had declined his proposal of marriage because of his blindness. We'll never know for sure, but this is his own account.

It is the quickest composition I ever achieved. It was done in three minutes. It seemed to me at the time as if someone was dictating the thought to me, and also giving the expression. There was so little sense of effort that I had a sensation of passiveness. I was sitting alone in my study in a state of great depression, caused by a real calamity. My hymn was the voice of my depression. It was not made for utilitarian purposes; it was wrung out spontaneously from the heart.

O Cross that liftest up my head,
I dare not ask to fly from thee:
I lay in dust life's glory dead,
And from the ground there blossoms
    red
Life that shall endless be.
    Revd George Matheson (1842–1906)

29 AUGUST

Martin Luther King was assassinated thirty years ago today, on 29 August 1963, just one day after he had made his famous speech at a Civil Rights march in Washington.

Now, I say to you today my friends, even though we face the difficulties of today and tomorrow, I still have a dream. It is a dream deeply rooted in the American dream. I have a dream that one day this nation will rise up and live out the true meaning of its creed: 'We hold these truths to be self-evident, that all men are created equal.'

I have a dream that one day on the red hills of Georgia the sons of former slaves and the sons of former slave owners will be able to sit down together at the table of brotherhood.

I have a dream that one day even the state of Mississippi, a state sweltering with the people's injustice, sweltering with the heat of oppression, will be transformed into an oasis of freedom and justice.

I have a dream that my four little children will one day live in a nation where they will not be judged by the colour of their skin but by the content of their character.

Martin Luther King (1929–68)

30 AUGUST

Every year more than 20,000 young Christians spend the August Bank Holiday at the Greenbelt Festival. They stay on a huge campsite — can you imagine what the 'queues for the loos' must be like? The three days are spent studying the Bible, listening to Christian speakers like Adrian Plass, worshipping, dancing, talking, arguing, clowning, and above all, playing and listening to very loud music!

Many young people don't want to come along to traditional church services, but it doesn't mean they aren't interested in religion. They like to go about it their own way. After all, they like different clothes, different food, different music, different television programmes — is it surprising they like different worship? Here's one of the songs they often sing when they worship.

> Colours of day dawn into the mind,
> The sun has come up, the night is
>   behind.
> Go down in the city, into the
>   street,
> And let's give the message to the
>   people we meet.
>
> *Chorus:*
> So light up the fire and let the
>   flame burn,

Open the doors, let Jesus return.
Take seeds of his Spirit, let the fruit
  grow,
Tell the people of Jesus, let his love
  show!

Susan McClellan, John Pac and
Keith Ryecroft
(Thank You Music, OUP, c 1974)

31 AUGUST
--

Today is the anniversary of another great man's
death — the Baptist preacher and writer, John
Bunyan. Do you remember how a postcard
from Bedford was the only letter that reached
Terry Waite during his five years as a hostage
in Beirut? The postcard showed John Bunyan in
Bedford prison, writing his book *The Pilgrim
Progress*. Terry kept it in his Bible until one day
the guards even took that away from him.

> Though with great difficulty I am
> got hither, yet now I do not repent
> me of all the trouble I have been at
> to arrive where I am. My sword, I
> give to him that shall succeed me in
> my pilgrimage, and my courage and
> skill to him that can get it. My
> marks and scars I carry with me, to
> be a witness for me, that I have
> fought his battles, who will now be

my rewarder . . . So he passed over,
and the trumpets sounded for him
on the other side.

John Bunyan (1628–88)
Mr Valiant-for-Truth in The Pilgrim's
Progress

SEPTEMBER

But it's a long long time
From May to December;
And the days grow short
When you reach September;
And these few precious days
I'd spend with you.
Maxwell Anderson (1888–1959)

1 SEPTEMBER

This is the month when everything in the countryside changes. The swallows and martins disappear. The leaves on the trees turn from green to red, yellow and gold; apples, pears and plums ripen in the orchards; sheep fields, woods and gardens secretly produce mushroooms overnight. Giant combine harvesters are at work on the hills, and for the next few weeks walkers and riders may roam freely over the harvested fields in late summer sunshine, across acres of 'stubble'.

> Season of mists and mellow
>   fruitfulness,
> Close bosom-friend of the
>   maturing sun;
> Conspiring with him how to load
>   and bless
> With fruit the vines that round the
>   thatch-eaves run.
> > *John Keats (1795–1821)*
> > *Ode to Autumn*

2 SEPTEMBER

When I'm not working, I like to walk round the shops with Scottie . . . We don't feel old — but oh dear! sometimes our legs do! We'll have a nice stroll down the road to Whitleys, where we always enjoy looking round, and sometimes having our lunch in Macdonalds. But as soon as we get back outside on the pavement, two sticks shoot up in the air and we both call out in unison, 'Taxi!' Taxi? It's only five-minutes' walk!

> These high wild hills and rough
>   uneven ways
> Draw out our miles and make them
>   wearisome.
>
> *William Shakespeare*
> *Richard II*

3 SEPTEMBER

I've said this many times — and I'll go on saying it, because God's listening and it's true. As soon as I start work — it can be acting in a play, or making a speech, or presenting the hymns on *Praise Be!* — it doesn't matter what it is, because as soon as I start I know that all my aches and pains will disappear. I say to Him Upstairs, 'Please let me be able to walk through this next scene without limping, and I won't grumble when it comes back afterwards.' He always keeps his side of the bargain, and I keep mine.

> Lay aside life-harming heaviness,
> And entertain a cheerful disposition.
>
> *William Shakespeare*
> *Richard II*

4 SEPTEMBER

Appropriately as summer comes to an end, we are recording another series of *Last of the Summer Wine*. The series has been going for nearly a quarter of a century. What can you say? It seems to touch a deep chord in people — these tales of three irrepressible, irresponsible old men wandering about the Yorkshire Moors, and the small group of strong Northern women who sit in everlasting judgement on them!

> When I do something right,
> nobody ever remembers it;
> When I do something wrong,
> nobody ever forgets it!

5 SEPTEMBER

It was Jack Rosenthal's play *Wide-eyed and Legless* on television tonight. I went to see the preview at BAFTA a few weeks ago and I cried all the way through. It's the saddest play I've ever been in. That's odd because it's full of funny lines, and the two main parts are played by Julie Walters and Jim Broadbent, both chiefly known as first-rate comic actors.

Julie Walters plays a woman suffering from a mysterious illness that no one can diagnose. I play her husband's, Jim Broadbent's, mother, whose gone a bit funny, but not enough to need locking away yet. There's a scene where she goes to see Julie Walters in hospital, and on her way down the ward she sees a woman in one of the beds who she recognizes. So she goes up to her and says, 'Now, I haven't seen you since, when was it?' and the woman in the bed says, 'Arthur's funeral'.

'Arthur's funeral!' she agrees, and after a little solemn pause enquires brightly, 'How is Arthur these days?'

The play makes you think, and I shall remember to pray from now on for people with confused minds and mysterious illnesses.

> The holier worship which he deigns
>   to bless
> Restores the lost, and binds the
>   spirit broken
> And feeds the widow and the
>   fatherless.
>   *John Greenleaf Whittier (1807–92)*

6 SEPTEMBER

A friend in Scotland telephoned to say that she has just counted forty swallows sitting on the telegraph wires that run across her garden. I suppose that means they will soon be leaving the North, on the first stage of their journey to Africa. When you see how tiny they are, it seems like a miracle doesn't it?

Swallows and martins are still busy feeding their young in the South of England, but I suppose they will all have gone from the nests here too by the end of October. I do miss them when they go.

> O Swallow, Swallow, flying, flying South,
> Fly to her, and fall upon her gilded eaves,
> And tell her, tell her, what I tell to thee.
>
> O tell her, Swallow, thou that knowest each,
> That bright and fierce and fickle is the South,
> And dark and true and tender is the North.
>
> *Alfred, Lord Tennyson 1809–92*
> *Song 3*

7 SEPTEMBER

It's not really like 'the good old days' at harvest time any more — is it? — when the whole village would join in. Nowadays the work is all done by one huge combine harvester, and a solitary man driving it. He sits high up in his little cabin, and you can sometimes spot his newspaper and sandwiches, or a mug of 'Cup-a-soup' balanced in front of the steering wheel!

> I made hay while the sun shone.
> My work sold.
> Now, if the harvest is over
> And the world cold,
> Give me the bonus of laughter
> As I lose hold.
>> *Sir John Betjeman (1906–84)*
>> *The Last Laugh*

8 SEPTEMBER

Just round the corner from us is the Notting Hill Gate parish of Father Michael Hollings. We don't see him so much as we used to on television these days, but he's still famous round these parts — for all the loving work he and all his parish does, helping people who are really at the bottom of the pile.

Today, like all Catholics, I'm sure they will be celebrating the birthday of the Blessed Virgin Mary.

> Ye who own the faith of Jesus
> Sing the wonders that were done,
> When the love of God the Father
> O'er our sin the victory won,
> When he made the Virgin Mary
> Mother of his only Son.
> Hail Mary, full of grace.

9 SEPTEMBER

The first frost is a reminder to start putting out food and water for our native garden birds, who won't be flying off to Africa and have a cold winter ahead of them. Like the rest of us!

It's nice to think that every time we throw out a few crumbs to the birds, we are doing exactly what Jesus said our heavenly Father does. What a very simple and lovely way for us to be Christians!

> Your heavenly Father feedeth them.
> *Matthew 6:26*

10 SEPTEMBER

We always like to put something out in the evenings for the neighbourhood hedgehogs, too, who trundle about the garden at this time of year, especially if you go outside after dark with a torch. They are busy building up nice fat tummies before their long winter sleep in the hollow of a tree, or buried snugly under a compost heap.

> Some nocturnal blackness, mothy
>   and warm,

When the hedgehog travels
  furtively over the lawn.
                    Thomas Hardy
                    Afterwards

11 SEPTEMBER
——

Here's my September haiku.

  Hallo, old hedgehog
  Trundling through moonlight. Have
  you
  Come for some cat food?

12 SEPTEMBER
——

As soon as I've finished recording the latest lot
of *Last of the Summer Wine* we're off! Scottie and
I are going on a Mediterranean cruise. Hurray!
It's another cruise arranged by SAGA especially
for retired people — so we know it will be good.
And it's time we got away again for a bit.

  The world is too much with us;
    late and soon,
  Getting and spending, we lay waste
    our powers:
  Little we see in Nature that is ours.
          William Wordsworth (1770–1850)

242

13 SEPTEMBER
— —

Postcard from Bonifacio, Corse. (La vieille ville
enfermée dans ses fortifications.)

> Lovely sail! Lovely ship! Blue skies!
> Sunshine! Wish you were here!!!!
> Love, Thor and Scottie

14 SEPTEMBER
— —

Apart from the beautiful places we visit, Scottie
and I aren't the sort of people who like to keep
themselves to themselves on holiday — we see
enough of one another all the rest of the year!
We enjoy making new friends and
acquaintances — and on these friendly SAGA
cruises you can't fail.

> From quiet homes and first
>   beginning,
> Out to the undiscovered ends,
> There's nothing worth the wear of
>   winning,
> But laughter and the love of
>   friends.
> > *Hilaire Belloc (1870–1953)*
> > *Dedicatory Ode*

15 SEPTEMBER

Battle of Britain Sunday

The Battle of Britain is not likely to be forgotten in a hurry, especially by the people of Kent or by the East Enders staying there to pick hops that summer of 1940. They all have their memories and stories to relive, of sheltering under trees to strip the hops while the aeroplane battle raged overhead. And although they were in great danger, their spirits were high.

Some young evangelical Christians are calling for a *new* Battle of Britain, a battle to win British people back to faith in the Lord.

What can we do to work God's work,
  to prosper and increase
The brotherhood of all mankind,
  the reign of the Prince of Peace?
What can we do to hasten the time
  the time that shall surely be,
When the earth shall be filled with the glory of God
  as the waters cover the sea?

March we forth in the strength of God
  with the banner of Christ unfurled,
That the light of the glorious

Gospel of truth
  may shine throughout the world.
Fight we the fight with sorrow and
  sin,
    to set their captives free,
That the earth shall be filled with
  the glory of God
    as the waters cover the sea.
A.C. Ainger (1841–1919)
'God is working his purpose out'

16 SEPTEMBER

September is the month when the Jewish New Year is celebrated at Rosh Hashanah, which, like our Easter, falls on a different day each year, depending on the moon. Whatever date Rosh Hashanah is celebrated, it is the beginning of ten days of repentance, and on the tenth day it's Yom Kippur — The Day of Atonement — the holiest day of the year. Jews neither eat nor drink today, and spend it in prayer, asking for forgiveness, and making their New Year resolutions.

Then said I, 'Woe is me! for I am undone; because I am a man of unclean lips, and I dwell in the midst of a people of unclean lips: for mine eyes have seen the King, the Lord of Hosts.'

Then flew one of the seraphims
unto me, having a live coal in his
hand, which he had taken with the
tongs from off the altar:
And he laid it upon my mouth, and
said, 'Lo, this hath touched thy lips;
and thine iniquity is taken away,
and thy sin purged.'
Also I heard the voice of the Lord,
saying, 'Whom shall I send, and
who will go for us?' Then said I,
'Here am I; send me.'

Isaiah 6:5–8

17 SEPTEMBER

In the garden young blackbirds are squabbling
for territory, and robins, their new red feathers
beginning to look quite sleek and smart, hop
hopefully about in search of friendly gardeners.

Proud Maisie is in the wood,
Waking so early,
Sweet robin sits in the bush,
Singing so rarely.

Sir Walter Scott (1771–1832)
The Heart of Midlothian

18 SEPTEMBER

This used to be our favourite time of the year for visiting Scottie's dad in Forfar, when he was still alive. Many's the time we've taken the high road — or the low road — to Scotland. The huge, still waters of the lochs, surrounded by heather-covered hills — no wonder it's called the Holy Land of the North! In September the purple heads of the native Scottish thistles turn white and fluffy, and the fields are full of swirling clouds of thistledown.

> Come again, with the feet
> That were light on the green as a
>   thistledown ball,
> And those mute ministrations to
>   one and to all
> Beyond a man's saying sweet.
>
> *Thomas Hardy*
> *After the Visit*

19 SEPTEMBER

Talking of Scotland, I wonder if you've come across the fairly recently published Glasgow Gospel? It's extracts from the gospels 'translated' into the Glasgow dialect by James Stuart. Here's an example.

Jesus then took his disciples tae
wan side an telt them, 'Ah'll soon
hiv tae leave ye aw — an though ye
search for me, ye canny follow
efter. So lissen, here's ma new
command for ye: ah want ye tae
love wan anither, jist the wey I
loved ye aw. That's the only wey
that ye can prove tae folk that you
are ma followers. There's nae
greater love in aw the world than
this: that a man should lay doon his
life for his freens. Don't let yet hert
get heavy. Trust oan God — *trust
oan me*. An mind, there are plenty
rooms in ma Faither's hoose. Ah'm
gaun there tae prepare a place for
everywan o ye. When things are ready,
ah'll come back for ye and we'll
aw be thegither wance mair . . .'.

John 13:33–35; 14:1@
James Stuart
The Glasgow Gospel

20 SEPTEMBER

As the swallows and martins prepare to depart,
we get some rather less welcome visitors: daddy
longlegs! Two are waltzing up and down my
kitchen window at this very moment as I write

to you, on their long spindly legs.

> He that lives in hope danceth
> without musick.
>> *George Herbert (1593–1633)*
>> *Outlandish Proverbs*

21 SEPTEMBER
— • —
St Matthew, the Apostle

St Matthew, the writer of the first gospel, is often pictured with a bag of coins or a money box, because he was a tax gatherer at Capernaum.

> And as Jesus passed forth from
> thence, he saw a man, named
> Matthew, sitting at the receipt of
> custom: and he saith unto him,
> 'Follow me'. And he arose and
> followed him.
>> *Matthew 9:9*

22 SEPTEMBER
— • —

I think the dreaded subject of money probably occupies theatrical people more than others, because there's no way for us to know from one year to the next how much work there will be,

how much we are going to earn . . . Or how
much tax we're going to have to pay, come to
that!

> We squander health in search of
>   wealth;
> We scheme and toil and save.
>
> Then squander wealth in search of
>   health,
> And only find a grave . . .
>
> *Anon.*

23 SEPTEMBER

You won't find out much about money in the
gospels, but Jesus did ask to be shown a penny
on one occasion, and used it as a teaching aid.

> And they asked him, saying,
> 'Master, we know that thou sayest
> and teachest rightly, neither
> acceptest thou the person of any,
> but teachest the way of God truly:
> Is it lawful for us to give tribute
> unto Caesar, or no?'
> But he perceived their craftiness,
> and said unto them, 'Why tempt ye
> me?
> Show me a penny. Whose image
> and superscription hath it?'

They answered and said, 'Caesar's.'
And he said unto them, 'Render
therefore unto Caesar the things
which be Caesar's, and unto God
the things which be God's.'

Luke 20:21–25

24 SEPTEMBER

We've found a cottage we might buy, and where do you think it is? Next-door to Jan and William! It belongs to such a nice couple — artists — but they want to move to somewhere with a bit more room. I'm saying my prayers about it, to see if it's meant to be, because I think it could be just right for us. And if I go first — well, you have to think of these things, don't you? — Scottie would have somewhere near Jan, where he could happily spend the rest of his life.

Isn't it funny how things work out? Only a few months ago I was feeling sorry about Jan and William leaving the Mill House, and now, with a bit of luck, we'll all be neighbours again!

Lord, help me to remember
that nothing is going to happen
    today
that you and I together can't
    handle!

Anon.

25 SEPTEMBER

—•—

If we do buy the cottage, this is the time of year
I shall most enjoy going down there — at the
end of the summer. The air is still summery and
warm, but not too hot. And in the mornings the
hedgerows will all be strung with spiders webs,
shining like diamonds in the early morning
dew.

> Hours fly, flowers die, love stays.
> *Words written on an old sundial.*

26 SEPTEMBER

—•—

In the countryside villagers and 'church mice'
will all be busily preparing for Harvest Festival.
The Harvest Supper Committee will be
working out how to serve a hundred hot
suppers in a church hall with no proper cooking
facilities — perhaps only a single Calor gas ring.
Someone will be out collecting raffle prizes, and
looking for volunteers to help with the washing
up!

The 'church mice' will be busy creating
wonderful arrangements around the altar with
chrysanthemums, dahlias, marigolds, Michael-
mas daisies and great swathes of branches of
autumn leaves; while all around them the

church steadily fills with baskets of giant marrows, prize-winning parsnips, carrots, tomatoes, apples, eggs, honey, bread and home-made marmalade.

> God is working his purpose out
>   as year succeeds to year,
> God is working his purpose out
>   and the time is drawing near;
> Nearer and nearer draws the time,
>   the time that shall surely be,
> When the earth shall be filled with
> the glory of God
>   as the waters cover the sea.
>   *A.C. Ainger (1841–1919)*

27 SEPTEMBER

When I was about five or six years old I went into business! I would take a bucket of peelings and exchange it for a cut apple at Houghton's, the greengrocers. The bucket of peelings was carried through the shop and emptied into a bin in their yard, to feed the pigs being reared for the butcher's shop next-door. When the empty bucket was returned, you were given a cut apple — an apple that had seen better days — or an over-ripe banana!

In the middle of our living-room table there was always a bowl of fruit — apples, polished and shining, and bananas, yellow, not black! So

I can only think that I went to the trouble of trading our bucket of peelings for a cut apple because I liked Billy Hadwen, who served at Houghton's. He wore a cap and a shirt with a brass collar stud showing, and was a very good, kind young man.

Many years later, I was guest star at the Royalty Theatre, and there was a press party held in the Dress Circle bar. During the chit-chat I saw a man having a quiet drink on the far side of the bar, and I kept thinking, I know that face. I very rarely forgot a face, although I often forget the name that goes with it. Eventually, the man made his way to where I was standing, and very shyly said, 'Hullo, Thora, love — what are you having?'

I looked into a kind, good face and — bingo! 'A cut apple, please, Mr Hadwen!' I said.

> Should auld acquaintance be forgot,
> And never brought to mind?
> . . . We'll take a cup o' kindness
> yet,
> For auld lang syne.
> *Robert Burns (1759–96)*

28 SEPTEMBER

We had a piano in our living room in Cheapside because my mother felt Nev and I would be more likely to do our piano practice, one hour a day each, if we were in the warm. A lot of pleasure was derived from the piano being on the spot, rather than in some freezing front room.

When my mother was ironing or sitting mending our clothes or socks, one of us would sit at the piano and accompany her while she sang. My favourite songs were 'O, where is my boy tonight?', 'Robin Adair', 'Sweet violets' and 'Sweet and Low'. This was because they were all in two sharps! In two sharps I was confident — I might even put a few twiddly bits in or a few runs!

> So now it is vain for the singer to
> burst into clamour
> With the great black piano
> appassionato. The glamour
> Of childish days is upon me, my
> manhood is cast
> Down in the flood of remembrance,
> I weep like a child for the past.
>> *D.H. Lawrence (1885–1930)*
>> *The Piano*

29 SEPTEMBER

St Michael and All Angels

And there was war in heaven: Michael and his angels fought

against the dragon; and the dragon
fought and his angels,
And prevailed not; neither was their
place found any more in heaven.
Revelation 12:7–8

Well, we can't all be heroes!

'Let's look for dragons,' I said to
    Pooh.
'Yes, let's,' said Pooh to me.
We crossed the river and found a
    few —
'Yes, those are dragons all right,'
    said Pooh,
'As soon as I saw their beaks I knew
That's what they are,' said Pooh,
    said he.
'That's what they are,' said Pooh.

'Let's frighten the dragons,' I said to
    Pooh.
'That's right', said Pooh to me.'
'I'm not afraid,' I said to Pooh.
And I held his paw and I shouted
    'Shoo!
Silly old dragons!' — and off they
    flew.
'I wasn't afraid,' said Pooh, said he,
'I'm never afraid with you.'
A.A. Milne (1882–1956)
Us Two

30 SEPTEMBER

The golden days of another summer are coming to a close. We've passed the autumn equinox, and I'm already noticing how much earlier the nights are drawing in.

> The golden age only comes to men
> when they have forgotten gold.
>   *G.K. Chesterton*

OCTOBER

No spring or summer hath
such grace,
As I have seen in one
autumnal face.
John Donne (1572–1631)
The Autumnal

1 OCTOBER

--

'Hares!' or should it be 'Rabbits!'? Do you know I've forgotten, but when we were children we always had to say — whichever it was — first, before we said anything else, on the first day of the month. I can't even remember why, but I suppose it was for luck. It's like all the old sayings. Why do we say 'Touch wood', for instance? Do you know? Neither do I. I think I'll do some looking up — and perhaps that'll be another book one day — *Thora's Little Book of Old Sayings!*

> Where is the life we have lost in
>   living?
> Where is the wisdom we have lost
>   in knowledge?
> Where is the knowledge we have
>   lost in information?
>
> > *T.S. Eliot*
> > *The Rock*

2 OCTOBER

--

Guardian Angels

I don't know whether it's right to believe this — but I think my mother watches over me, like a guardian angel.

For instance, on the second night of our

261

cruise this year, I was tidying my hair before going into the dining room, and I saw in the mirror that my ring had gone. It was an engagement ring, which I wear on my little finger now, with three keepers, because it's just a bit too big.

I was on my knees, feeling all over the floor. Nothing. I asked the cabin maid for a torch. Nothing. The plumber came and checked the drains from the loo and the sink. Nothing. I love it dearly, that ring, more than more expensive rings I've got. So I said a quick prayer to my mother.

Two nights before we went home, I heard and saw something drop in the middle of the cabin floor, between our two beds. I saw it drop just the last three inches. My ring!

I'm still sure my mother found it for me. Does that sound daft to you?

> The loveliest masterpiece of the heart of God is the heart of a mother.
>
> *St Thérèse of Lisieux (1837–97)*

3 OCTOBER

Faith isn't a list of propositions you are supposed to take down in your little notebook and tick off. It's poetry, and fumbling, and seeing through the mists.

Our birth is but a sleep and a
  forgetting:
The Soul that rises with us, our
  life's star,
Hath had elsewhere its setting,
And cometh from afar;
Not in entire forgetfulness,
And not in utter nakedness,
But trailing clouds of glory do we
  come
From God, who is our home.
Heaven lies about us in our infancy!
Shades of the prison-house begin to
  close
Upon the growing boy,
But he beholds the light, and
  whence it flows,
He sees it in his joy;
The youth, who daily farther from
  the east
Must travel, still is Nature's priest,
And by the vision splendid
Is on his way attended;
At length the man perceives it die
  away,
And fade into the light of common
  day.

William Wordsworth
Intimations of Immortality (1807)

4 OCTOBER

— —

St Francis

I've heard of so many places now where 4 October, or the nearest Sunday, has become 'Animal Sunday' — as a way of commemorating the saint who loved and respected all created things, St Francis of Assissi.

Everyone is invited to bring their pet animal to church. What an assembly! And what a cacophony of barking, growling and mewing, even clucking, if a disapproving hen is present! Goldfish swim gloomily round in the small jars they've been transferred to from their nice big bowls at home. Mice and guinea pigs hide rustling in their straw. You even hear of people bringing goats, sheep, donkeys and ponies to church! It's all very loving, and a reminder that animals have always had an important part to play in the mystery of the Christian story.

> Enough for him, whom cherubim
> Worship night and day,
> A breastful of milk,
> And a mangerful of hay:
> Enough for him, whom angels
> Fall down before,
> The ox and ass and camel
> Which adore.
> *Christina Rossetti (1830–94)*

5 OCTOBER

Speaker's Corner, in Hyde Park, is round the corner from us; and the West London Methodist Mission at Hinde Street isn't far away. So it won't surprise you to learn that we are great admirers of Lord Donald Soper.

This year he was celebrating his ninetieth birthday. So on that Sunday in January, *after* he had finished his regular stint in Hyde Park, kindly note — giving as good as he got to the hecklers, who usually end up becoming his greatest fans — he came along to the West London Mission for a special *Songs of Praise,* and chose all the hymns.

For the first time, 'The Old Rugged Cross' wasn't the most requested hymn on *Praise Be!* this year, because it was supplanted by one Lord Soper chose for his birthday. He said he'd liked it since he was a boy, when he had always wished he could have been one of the children who came to Jesus and felt the touch of his hand on his head. Dear me, so many of you wrote to tell me that you had always wished that too!

> I think when I read that sweet
>   story of old
> When Jesus was here among men,
> How he called little children as
>   lambs to his fold,
> I should like to have been with
>   them then;

I wish that his hands had been
   placed on my head,
That his arm had been thrown
   around me,
And that I might have seen his kind
   look when he said,
'Let the little ones come unto me.'
                    Jemima Luke (1813–1906)

6 OCTOBER
— —

If you go out walking in the London parks in
the late afternoon or early evening at this time
of year and look up — you'll see flocks of geese
flying overhead. I don't know where they go to,
but every afternoon skeins of five or six take off
from the park lakes and disappear over the
London chimney-tops in that familiar V
formation.

   I'll love you till the ocean
   Is folded and hung up to dry
   And the seven stars go squawking
   Like geese about the sky.
                    W.H. Auden
                    As I Walked Out One Evening

7 OCTOBER

All over the countryside the harvesters have left their big circular rolls of straw lying on the stubble. Round woolly sheep nibble at turnips. Have you ever noticed, the sheep and the straw rolls are almost exactly the same colour and shape — except the sheep have legs — fat and roly-poly in the autumn sunshine?

> Thou crownest the year with thy
> goodness; and thy clouds drop
> fatness.
> They shall drop upon the dwellings
> of the wilderness; and the little hills
> shall rejoice on every side.
> The folds shall be full of sheep; the
> valleys also shall stand so thick
> with corn, that they shall laugh and
> sing.
>
> *Psalm 65:11–13*
> *Book of Common Prayer*

8 OCTOBER

If you go down in the woods today . . . you may hear the bark of a startled pheasant cock; or see a pair of herons rise slowly from the side of a stream, where they have been fishing, and glide silently away on graceful wings.

It was my thirtieth year to heaven
Woke to my hearing from harbour
  and neighbour wood
And the mussel pooled and the heron
Priested shore.
Dylan Thomas (1914–53)
Poem in October

9 OCTOBER

I wonder if our politicians aren't becoming rather too fond of being seen on television? It's almost as though people nowadays think that you can only do any good if you are 'famous'. Tommy rot!

> The growing good of the world is
> partly dependent on unhistoric acts;
> and that things are not so ill with
> you and me as they might have
> been, is half owing to the number
> who lived faithfully a hidden life,
> and rest in unvisited tombs.
> *George Eliot (1819–80)*
> *Middlemarch*

10 OCTOBER

It's a long time since Scottie and I last made the journey 'over the border', but this is the very best time of year to visit the highlands and islands in the west of Scotland if you're ever going to.

You have to see it to understand how beautiful light can be. You drive through miles and miles of hills in every shade of brown, gold and purple. Rain brings silver cascades of water flooding down the mountainsides, and rainbows come and go across the lochs. The high mountain tops are sometimes capped with snow and frost, but down below the air still holds the last warmth of summer.

You may not see an eagle — but you get the feeling that eagles see you. It must surely be the only wilderness left in Britain.

> I will lift up mine eyes unto the
> hills, from whence cometh my help.
> My help cometh from the Lord,
> which made heaven and earth.
> *Psalm 121:1–2*

11 OCTOBER

For anyone who wants to climb or walk in the mountains, they couldn't prepare themselves better than by reading these Ten Commandments of Climbing, written by Hamish Brown.

1. Thou shalt prepare thoroughly before starting.

2. Thou shalt start early.
3. Thou shalt set out properly equipped.
4. Thou shalt choose thy company with care.
5. Thou shalt not destroy anything which is thy neighbour's.
6. Thou shalt often keep silence to hear the mountain speak.
7. Thou shalt leave no sign of thy passing.
8. Thou shalt remember others in their strength or weakness.
9. Thou shalt bend to the weather and be strong.
10. Thou shalt be humble and praise God.

Hamish Brown

12 OCTOBER

There was an avenue of beech trees along a long straight road which we used to drive down whenever we went to Benenden in Kent, to visit Daisy at school. In October the leaves were gold, and as we drove under the beautiful, arching branches we always used to say, 'Oh! It's like being in a cathedral.'

Then came the Great Gale, in October 1987, and nearly every single tree fell. They've planted a new tree beside each one that fell, and in twenty years or so other families will drive along there, just as Scottie, Jan and I have done so often, and I hope they'll turn to one another and say, 'It's just like being in a cathedral!'

Be still, and know that I am God.
Psalm 46:10

13 OCTOBER
— —

When Moses saw a bush on fire on Mount Horeb, perhaps the reason the bush was not consumed was because it threw out its seeds, to create new life.

> And the angel of the Lord appeared
> unto Moses in a flame of fire out of
> the midst of a bush: and he looked,
> and behold, the bush burned with
> fire, and the bush was not
> consumed.
>
> *Exodus 3:2*

14 OCTOBER
— —

When Malcolm Muggeridge interviewed Mother Teresa of Calcutta on television, many years ago, he asked her whether, in view of the commonly held opinion that there are too many people in India, it was worthwhile trying to salvage a few abandoned children who might otherwise be expected to die of neglect or malnutrition. He wrote afterwards, in his book *Something Beautiful for God:*

It was a point so remote from her whole way of looking at life that she had difficulty in grasping it. The notion that there could in any circumstances be too many children was, to her, as inconceivable as suggesting that there are too many bluebells in the woods or stars in the sky. In the film we made there is a shot of Mother Teresa holding a tiny baby girl in her hands; so minute that her very existence seemed like a miracle. As she holds this child, she says in a voice, and with an expression, of exaltation most wonderful and moving: 'See! there's life in her!'

Malcolm Muggeridge (1903–90)
Something Beautiful for God

15 OCTOBER

St Teresa of Avila

The Mother Teresa of the sixteenth century was a Spanish Carmelite nun. She was known by the clerical authorities — many of whom didn't approve of her at all — as the 'roving nun' because she was always on the move, opening new houses and filling them with nuns who were inspired by her ideals. She wrote a book of prayers that reflected her spiritual journey, called *The Book of God's Mercies.*

Her influence — like that of our own Mother Teresa — on the spiritual lives of Christians of all denominations is immeasurable. Teresa is the saint of sound common sense, and strong ideals, and great good humour.

> O my Lord, since it seems you are
> determined to save me, I ask that
> you may do so quickly. And since
> you have decided to dwell within
> me, I ask that you clean your
> house, wiping away all the grime of
> sin.
>
> *St Teresa of Avila (1515–82)*

16 OCTOBER

Week of Prayer for World Peace

I can't think of a better private prayer, for this week, than the prayer of St Francis.

> Lord, make me an instrument of
>   your peace.
> Where there is hatred — let me sow
>   love;
> Where there is injury, pardon;
> Where there is doubt, faith;
> Where there is despair — let me
>   give hope;

Where there is darkness, light;
Where there is sadness, joy.
O divine master, grant that I may
    not try
to be comforted, but to comfort;
not to be understood, but to
    understand;
not to be loved, but to love;
Because it is in giving that we
    receive,
in forgiving that we are forgiven,
and in dying that we are born — to
    eternal life.

17 OCTOBER

After last winter I didn't think things could get worse in Bosnia — but they aren't getting any better. People who were neighbours and friends are now forced to be enemies, and everyone lives in danger of being killed by a sniper's bullet if they leave their homes — even children playing.

Mother Teresa comes from Yugoslavia — if only there were more like her still there . . .

Our works of love are nothing but
works of peace. Let us do them
with greater love and efficiency —
each in her own or his own work
in daily life; in your home — in

your neighbourhood. It is always the same Christ who says:

'I was hungry — not only for food, but for peace that comes from a pure heart.

'I was thirsty — not for water, but for peace that satiates the passionate thirst of passion for war.

'I was naked — not for clothes, but for that beautiful dignity of men and women for their bodies.

'I was homeless — not for a shelter made of bricks, but for a heart that understands, that covers, that loves.'

Let us radiate the peace of God and so light his light and extinguish in the world and in the hearts of all men all hatred, and love for power.

Mother Teresa (b.1910)
From a letter to the co-workers

18 OCTOBER

St Luke

Because St Luke, who wrote the third gospel and the book of Acts, was a doctor, we are asked to make a special point of remembering doctors, nurses and everyone connected with medicine and healing in our prayers today. Here

is a prayer by William Barclay that fits the bill
I reckon.

O God,
I thank you for Jesus, the Good
Physician.
I thank you that he restored health
to men's bodies
    and sanity to their minds.
I thank you that he cared for all
who were in pain
    of body and in distress of mind.
I thank you for all doctors who
follow in his steps:
    for all who have studied and
toiled and experimented
      to find a cure for disease;
    for all who have risked their life
and their health
      that others might be healed;
    for all who have skill to heal the
body;
    for all who have patience to
minister to minds which
      have lost their balance;
    for those whose quiet, calm
strength stills men's
      fears when they are worried and
in pain.
Give to all engaged in the work of
healing

the joy of knowing that they do
the work
of Jesus, the Good Physician.

William Barclay
Prayers for Help and Healing

19 OCTOBER

Jan and William are now settled into their new
home, and Jan says it's the house of her dreams.
Being Jan, she has quickly made good friends
in the neighbourhood, but I know she also still
goes back to our old village church sometimes
— because when you've become part of the life
of a church, it's almost like a second family, isn't
it?

And so I give you our toast. From
that young man upstairs who has
had the impudence to make me a
great-uncle, to Mother and Father
on their Golden Wedding; through
four generations of us, and to those
who have gone, and those who are
to come. To the family — that dear
octopus from whose tentacles we
never quite escape, nor, in our
inmost hearts, ever quite wish to.

Dodie Smith (1896–1990)
Dear Octopus (1938)

20 OCTOBER

I left school at fourteen, so you might know I've never been to university. But I've got an *honorary* degree — I've been made Doctor of Literature at the University of Lancaster.

As Scottie and Jan accompanied me to the Graduation Hall in Lancaster to receive my honorary degree, I was wondering what I should say to all the young new graduates, and to Princess Alexandra, who as Chancellor of the University would be doing the presentation . . . Then, as we were very nearly there, we drove past a place I hadn't seen in fifty years, and I suddenly knew exactly what I was going to tell them — the story of the Lancaster and District Co-op Dinner and Dance, held annually in the Ashton Hall.

Tickets were 2/6 (including dinner). When my best friend, Peg, and I arrived, wearing our first grown-up ballgowns, people were being seated for the dinner so we took our places, very excited and expecting a good evening. The soup was served — cream of mushroom. As the waiter started to put a plate of soup in front of me, he caught his elbow on the chair-back of the person next to me and . . . Yes, the entire portion of soup, right into my lap!

It was very hot, and went straight through my satin dress and real silk stockings, and I let out a yell. I jumped up, and Peg rushed after me into the Ladies' Room. In those days there were no little piles of paper towels, just a rather damp roller towel on the back of the door — too high up to be of any use. We pulled my dress off to rinse the soup off the front, and then we had to mop it dry with our two little lace-edged hankies. By now tears were very near, but I tidied up my hair and we bravely went back to our dinner places.

As I drove by, fifty years on, with my husband and daughter in our chauffeur-driven limousine, to be made a Doctor of Literature for services to Lancashire, I thought, well it sort of evens things up, somehow . . . .

> Our deeds still travel with us from afar,
> And what we have been makes us what we are.
> > *George Eliot (1819–80)*
> > *Middlemarch*

21 OCTOBER

Our grandson, James, is the spitting image of Scottie — same ears, same sort of nose, same little cleft in his chin and the same sort of expressive eyes as Scottie. Jan is also the spitting image of her daddy and Daisy takes after *her* father's side of the family; but nobody, but nobody, is the spitting image of me! Unless, that is, you count the 10,000 women who all claim that *they* are — and send me photographs to prove it! But they aren't relatives — so they can't blame me!

Does anyone recognize these lines? I can't remember where they come from — I'd love to know.

> And mountain grasses cannot help
>   retain
> The imprint where the mountain
>   hare has lain.

Anon.

22 OCTOBER
——

Here's an extract from another *Little Grey Rabbit* storybook — written for children, but I so love reading them still!

Hare has come racing home 'like the north wind' to tell little Grey Rabbit and Squirrel about a party in progress down at the farmhouse. They've never seen a party, so they decide to go and peep in.

> They ran across the drive to the
> lawn, and stood under the juniper-
> bush, staring in the twilight at the
> darkened house. 'I can't see
> anything,' murmured Grey Rabbit
> sadly.
>
> 'Nor I,' muttered Squirrel,

running up the bush and down again.

'They've shuttered the windows,' cried Hare, disappointedly, and they all gazed unhappily at the barred shutters. Little sounds of merriment, squeals and cries of joy came from the hidden room, and Grey Rabbit gasped as she listened.

Hare walked slowly round the corner of the gable, and Squirrel and Grey Rabbit trailed after. Then Hare gave a shrill cry. 'Here's a little window they've forgotten,' said he. 'Come and look here!' Hare stood on tiptoes, Squirrel climbed a rose-bush and little Grey Rabbit scrambled on top of a wheelbarrow. In the warm bright room they could see little boys and girls in party frocks and Sunday suits, playing Blind Man's Buff, and Hunt the Thimble, and Musical Chairs . . .

. . . Then the children trooped off to another room for tea, and the animals only got a glimpse of the gay table through the open door, when a hand appeared and closed the shutter. They were left out in the cold . . .

. . . 'What do you think of that?'

asked Hare, turning a somersault. 'I found it! It was my discovery!'

'It was very clever of you,' said Squirrel, but little Grey Rabbit said nothing. She sat in the wheelbarrow staring at the blank window. She took little short breaths and her eyes shone.

'Why don't you speak, Grey Rabbit?' cried Hare impatiently, and Grey Rabbit leapt down and trotted silently by his side. 'Didn't you like it? Wasn't it wonderful?'

'Yes,' whispered Grey Rabbit, 'I was thinking, and wondering, and wishing. That's all.'

Alison Uttley
Little Grey Rabbit's Party

23 OCTOBER

On the news today — another IRA bomb. This time it was in a Belfast fish shop. Nine people, including the person who planted the bomb, were killed. May God forgive them.

Forgive, like the Lord that you love — or become like the enemy you hate.

Cardinal Gordon Gray

24 OCTOBER

End of British Summertime

The clocks have gone back one hour. A friend of ours has a rather absent-minded, elderly father living on his own, so at eleven o'clock this morning, she telephoned to remind him about the extra hour. 'I know. I've done it,' he told her cheerfully. 'I'm just eating my lunch.'

> If neither brass nor marble can
>   withstand
> The mortal force of Time's
>   destructive hand;
> If mountains sink to vales, if cities
>   die,
> And lessening rivers mourn their
>   fountains dry:
> When my old cassock (said a Welsh
>   divine)
> Is out at elbows — why should I
>   repine?
> > *Dr Jonathan Swift (1667–1745)*
> > *The Power of Time*

25 OCTOBER

On every tall tree or telegraph pole there's a thrush or a blackbird singing its heart out. It's as if they share our sad feeling now that summer is over, and the swallow and martins are leaving us for another year. A robin stands sentinel on a molehill, singing a melancholy song and puffing out his chest, like a thumb-print of blood.

> The red-breast whistles from a
>   garden-croft;
> And gathering swallows twitter in
>   the skies.
>
> *John Keats* (1795—1821)
> Ode to Autumn

26 OCTOBER

On the radio recently, Benjamin Whitrow has been reading from the diaries of the Reverend Gilbert White, the eighteenth—century country parson and naturalist. Do you know them? They are marvellous!

> If a masterly landscape painter was
> to take our hanging woods in their
> autumnal colours, persons
> unacquainted with the country
> would object to the strength and
> deepness of the tints, and would
> pronounce, at an exhibition, that
> they were heightened and shaded
> beyond nature.
>
> *Gilbert White (1720–93)*
> *October 1783 (Hampshire)*

27 OCTOBER

—-—

Gilbert White had a fixed idea, after noticing some house-martins flying through the village in November, that at least some birds didn't migrate — but became dormant, like insects! He went on the track of his 'hibernating house-martins'!

As my principal object was to discover the place of their roosting, I . . . was much pleased to find that, for several evenings together, just at a quarter past five in the afternoon, they all scudded away in great haste towards the south-east, and darted down among the low shrubs above the cottages at the end of the hill . . .

. . . I have only to add that were the bushes, which cover some acres, and are not my own property, to be grubbed and carefully examined, probably those late broods, and perhaps the whole aggregate body of the house-martins of this district, might be found there, in different secret dormitories; and that so far from withdrawing into warmer climes, it would appear that they never depart 300 yards from the village.

Gilbert White
The Natural History of Selborne
Letter, October 1781

28 OCTOBER

October Haiku
Safe in the shadows
Mice twitch. Owl wings fan the
night
There's a hunter's moon.

29 OCTOBER

After a beautiful day, it gets dark quickly now
the clocks have changed.

> Eternal Ruler of the ceaseless round
>   of circling planets singing on
>   their way;
> Guide of the nations from the night
>   profound
>   into the glory of the perfect day;
> Rule in our hearts, that we may
>   ever be
> Guided and strengthened and
>   upheld by thee.
>   *J.W. Chadwick (1840–1904)*

30 OCTOBER

Someone has sent me a newspaper article
written by Paul Heiney — whose lovely,
traditional farm I visited this spring — and in

it he says that, 'we were knocked out by Thora, so we've named one of our baby pigs after her . . .'

Now I call that a great compliment . . . Yes it is.

> The Owl and the Pussy-Cat went
>   to sea
> In a beautiful pea-green boat.
> They took some honey, and plenty
>   of money,
> Wrapped up in a five-pound note.
> The Owl looked up to the stars
>   above
> And sang to a small guitar,
> 'Oh lovely Pussy! O Pussy, my
>   love,
> What a beautiful Pussy you are.'
>   *Edward Lear (1812–88)*

31 OCTOBER

Halloween

In the old Celtic calendar the last night of October was 'old year night', when witches were abroad. The Christian Church changed it to Eve of All-Hallows, but children still like to scare each other with tales of the old witches.

Our part of rural Sussex became quite notorious because of stories going round about witches and strange, black magic rites. Perhaps there was a bit of truth in it — but most of it was people enjoying a scary tale. You could almost think you were back in the Middle Ages!

In those days Bishop Peter Ball was our Bishop, and he helped people to see things in proportion. When someone said to him once, 'Don't you ever feel nervous, Bishop Peter, walking about on your own in remote places, with such funny goings on?' He answered, 'Nervous? On my own? Why, there are so many angels about, I have to push them to one side to get along the lane!'

> Teach me, my God and King,
> In all things thee to see;
> And what I do in anything
> To do it as for thee.
>
> A man that looks on glass,
> On it may stay his eye;
> Or, if he pleaseth, through it pass,
> And then the heaven espy.
> *George Herbert (1593–1633)*

NOVEMBER

A Month of Memories

~ ~

No warmth, no cheerfulness, no
  healthful ease,
No comfortable feel in any
  member —
No shade, no shine, no butterflies,
  no bees,
No fruits, no flowers, no leaves,
  no birds, —
November!
  Thomas Hood (1799–1845)
  No

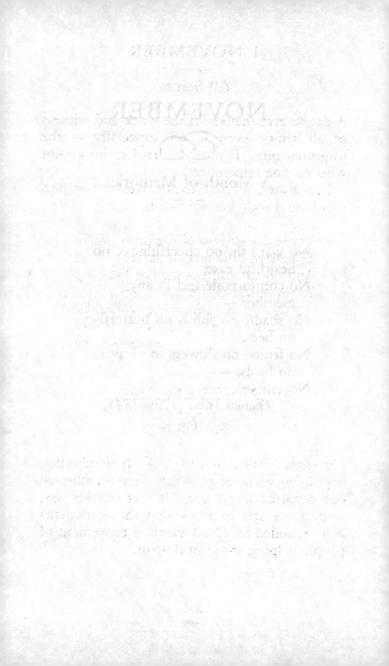

1 NOVEMBER

All Saints

A day to give thanks for the work and witness of all saints, even — no, especially — the forgotten ones. It must be hard to be a saint who no one remembers!

I've always liked Charles Wesley's *original* words to a well-known hymn.

> Come, let us join our friends above
> That have obtained the prize,
> And on the eagle wings of love
> To joy celestial rise.
>
> *Charles Wesley (1707–88)*
> *usually known as 'Let saints on earth*
> *in concert sing'*

2 NOVEMBER

All Souls

November is a month for remembering, beginning with today, when we remember all our departed loved ones. It was on this day, forty years ago in 1953, that the Samaritans were founded by Chad Varah, a movement of people helping those in despair.

291

I have taken life on the sad side,
and it has helped me to understand
many, many failures, many utter
ruins.

Abbe Havelin (1838–1910)

3 NOVEMBER

When Mother Teresa of Calcutta received her
Nobel Prize in 1979, in her acceptance speech
she said that the poverty of the West is much
more difficult to remove than the poverty of the
Third World.

When I pick up a person from the
streets hungry, I give him a plate of
rice, a piece of bread, and I have
satisfied that hunger; but a person
that is shut out, that feels
unwanted, unloved, terrified, the
person that has been thrown out of
society — how much more difficult
it is to remove that hunger.

Mother Teresa

4 NOVEMBER

A letter has come today, from the Series
Producer of *Songs of Praise*, telling me that they
won't be wanting me to do *Praise Be!* any more.

Praise Be! has become a big part of our family's life over the past seventeen years — especially since we've been making the programmes at Jan's home, where everyone seems to get roped in! And wherever I go, the people I meet are always asking, 'When's your hymn series coming back, Thora?'

Above all, no one will ever know how much I'm going to miss the letters, only the elderly ladies who are going to miss me going into their homes on Sunday night.

> God, grant us the serenity to accept the things we cannot change; the courage to change the things we must; and the wisdom to know the difference.
> *Reinhold Niebuhr (1892–1971)*

5 NOVEMBER

It's Guy Fawkes' night — but here's something better to remember than 'Gunpowder, treason and plot'.

> Remember, Christian Soul, that thou hast this day and every day of thy life:
> God to glorify. Jesus to imitate. A soul to save. A body to mortify. Sins to repent of. Virtues to

acquire. Hell to avoid. Heaven to
gain. Eternity to prepare for. Time
to profit by. Neighbours to edify.
The world to despise. Devils to
combat. Passions to subdue. Death,
perhaps, to suffer. Judgement to
undergo.

St Augustine of Hippo

6 NOVEMBER
— —

In all the debates and discussions we hear today
about the pros and cons of teaching religion to
children, I've never heard anyone speak or write
more sense than that clever man, who wrote the
Narnia stories for children, C.S. Lewis.

If we had noticed that the young
people of the present day found it
harder and harder to get the right
answers to sums, we should
consider that this had been
adequately explained the moment
we discovered that schools had for
some years ceased to teach
arithmetic.
After that discovery, we should
turn a deaf ear to people who
offered explanations of a vaguer
and larger kind — people who said
that the influence of Einstein had

294

sapped the ancestral belief in fixed numerical relations, or that gangster films had undermined the desire to get the right answers, or that the evolution of consciousness was now entering on its post-arithmetical phase.

Where a clear and simple explanation completely covers the facts, no other explanation is in court. If the younger generation have never been told what the Christians say and never heard any arguments in defence of it, then their agnosticism or indifference is fully explained. . . . And having discovered that the cause of their ignorance is lack of instruction, we have also discovered the remedy. There is nothing in the nature of the younger generation which incapacitates them for receiving Christianity. If anyone is prepared to tell them, they are apparently ready to hear.

C.S. Lewis (1898–1963)

7 NOVEMBER

I don't know when or where this next piece of advice originally came from, but with growing concern about young children committing dreadful crimes today, I think it will strike a chord.

How to Make a Child into a Delinquent: Twelve Easy Rules

1. Begin at infancy to give the child everything he wants.
2. When he picks up bad language, laugh at him.
3. Never give him any spiritual training. Wait until he is twenty-one, and then let him 'decide for himself'.
4. Avoid the use of the word 'wrong'. It may develop a guilt complex.
5. Pick up everything he leaves lying around, books, shoes, clothes.
6. Let him read any printed matter he can get his hands on.
7. Quarrel frequently in the presence of your children. In this way they will not be too shocked when the home is broken up later.
8. Give a child all the spending money he wants. Why should he have things as tough as you had them?
9. Satisfy his every craving for food, drink and comfort. Denial may lead to harmful frustration.
10. Take his part against neighbours, teachers, policemen.
11. When he gets into real trouble, apologize for

yourself by saying, 'I could never do anything with him.'

12. Prepare yourself for a life of grief.

Anon.

8 NOVEMBER

I must be one of British Rail's best customers — especially over the past nearly twenty years when I've been regularly travelling between London and Leeds for the various comedy series I've had the pleasure of being in: *In Loving Memory, Alleluia!* and *Last of the Summer Wine* — all set in the North of England.

Trains have changed a lot in my lifetime, but I still find it a romantic way to travel. Do you remember how there always used to be a big leather strap fixed to the big windows for opening and shutting them? I always had to get someone else to help me with it — but now I rather miss them . . . I don't know why.

North, north, north,
To the country of the Clyde and the
   Firth of Forth.

This is the night mail crossing the
   border,
Bringing the cheque and the postal
   order,
Letters for the rich, letters for the poor,

The shop at the corner and the girl
   next-door.

W.H. Auden
Night Mail (1935)

9 NOVEMBER
— —

By the time you are reading this you may also
have read my *Little Book of Home Truths* —
because as I write this, a letter has come from
the publisher's to tell me that the 'page proofs'
are on their way for me to check and correct.
I shall enjoy that! One of my favourite 'home
truths' is for us older people, and I ended the
book with it.

Remember — we don't stop doing
things because we have grown old —
we grow old because we have stopped
doing things!

10 NOVEMBER
— —

Every year on Remembrance Day there are the
dead of more wars to remember: the First and
Second World Wars, Suez, Vietnam, the
Falklands, the Gulf, Bosnia . . . There's also all
the ordinary people, children and women as
well as soldiers, who have been killed in
something worse than a war — the terrorism

that goes on in, and comes out of, Northern Ireland.

> Comfort every sufferer
> Watching late in pain;
> Those who plan some evil
> From their sin restrain.
> *S. Baring-Gould (1834–1924)*
> *'Now the day is over'*

11 NOVEMBER

Remembrance Day
75th Armistice Day

I was at school on the very first Armistice Day, when at the eleventh hour of the eleventh day of the eleventh month we all stood by our desks like statues, absolutely silent, for two minutes . . . it felt like about a year! Every year on Remembrance Day everything stopped — all traffic, schools, factories — *everything* — for two minutes. Bus drivers and their passengers would get out and stand to attention beside the buses in the middle of Oxford Street!

These days Scottie and I watch the Cenotaph service on the television, especially the brave march past of the 'boys' of the old brigade, men and women, wearing their rows of medals on their chests with so much pride. There are no dry eyes in our house, I promise you!

We give back to you, O God, those
whom you gave to us. You did not
lose them when you gave them to
us, and we do not lose them by
their return to you. Your dear Son
has taught us that life is eternal and
love cannot die. So death is only a
horizon, and a horizon is only the
limit of our sight. Open our eyes to
see more clearly, and draw us closer
to you that we may know that we
are nearer to our loved ones, who
are with you.

You have told us that you are
preparing a place for us: prepare us
also for that happy place, that
where you are we may also be
always, O dear Lord of life and
death.

William Penn (1644–1718)

12 NOVEMBER

You don't have to be a pacifist or a Buddhist to
pray for peace. We all pray for peace.

Lead me from death
to Life, from falsehood to Truth

Lead me from despair
to Hope, from fear to Trust

Lead me from hate
to Love, from war to Peace

Let Peace fill our heart,
our world, our universe.

Satish Kumar
adopted by the Prayer for Peace
movement, 1981

13 NOVEMBER

Here's a haiku for November, the month of
remembering. I didn't write this — it's a nice
one by the Japanese poet, Issa.

Visiting the graves . . .
Trotting on to show the way . . .
Old family dog.

14 NOVEMBER

It's seventy years since John Reith became the
Managing Director of the BBC. By all accounts
he was not an easy man, nor a happy one
personally, but on the day after he died, in June
1971, *The Times* concluded a leading article
with not a bad epitaph:

The corporate personality of the
BBC still gets, and will continue to
get, a twitch on the thread from

301

that angular Scots engineer, of
unabashed earnestness and
unbending strength, who, having
survived a sniper's bullet in 1915,
felt himself to be elected by
Providence to do something great
in the world. He did.

15 NOVEMBER

Someone else who hasn't been universally
popular, but whom I personally admire very
much, is Mary Whitehouse. I was sorry to read
today that she is retiring from the moral crusade
she began in 1964. It's through her work and
energy that we have the Broadcasting Standards
Council. Her National Viewers and Listeners
Association has been the bane of many a 'free-
thinker', who wanted to broadcast swear words
and rude pictures in the name of 'Art' — and
the champion of countless gentle souls, who
didn't want their homes and their children's
minds polluted with violence and porno-
graphy.

As my poor father used to say
In 1863,
Once people start on all this Art
Goodbye, moralitee!
And what my father used to say

Is good enough for me.

A.P. Herbert (1890–1971)
Ballads for Broadbrows
'Lines for a worthy person'

16 NOVEMBER

St Margaret of Scotland

As I write this, it is the 90th anniversary of this great Christian Queen, who loved the poor. And back into my head has come a song we used to sing at school, John Keats' poem *Meg Merrilies* . . . .. I think I can still remember most of the words.

> Old Meg she was a gipsy,
> And lived upon the moors;
> Her bed it was the brown heath
>   turf,
> And her house was out of doors.
> Her apples were swart blackberries,
> Her currants, pods o' broom;
> Her wine was dew of the wild
>   white rose,
> Her book a churchyard tomb.
>
> Her brothers were the craggy hills,
> Her sisters larchen trees;
> Alone with her great family
> She lived as she did please.

No breakfast had she many a morn,
No dinner many a noon,
And 'stead of supper, she would
    stare
Full hard against the moon.

But every morn, of woodbine fresh
She made her garlanding;
And, every night, the dark glen yew
She wove, and she would sing.
And with her fingers, old and
    brown,
She plaited mats of rushes,
And gave them to the cottagers
She met among the bushes.

Old Meg was brave as Margaret
    Queen,
And tall as Amazon:
An old red blanket cloak she wore,
A chip-hat had she on.
God rest her aged bones
    somewhere —
She died full long agone!
                    John Keats (1795–1821)

17 NOVEMBER

— - —

Women Priests

I'm very glad to read in my paper today that at
long last, after a year's toing and froing, women

are to be ordained as priests in the Church of England. In fact — by the time you are reading this — some of us will already have a woman as vicar — D.V. Women have always been trusted with the most important job of all — teaching children about Jesus, at home and in Sunday School. If they can do that, surely to God they can play their part in guiding and leading the rest of us on our Christian journey.

> . . . It was Mary Magdalene, and
> Joanna, and Mary the mother of
> James and other women that were
> with them, which told these things
> unto the apostles.
> And their words seemed to them as
> idle tales, and they believed them not.
> *Luke 24:10–11*

18 NOVEMBER
--

This is the season of Divali — the Hindu New Year festival — a time of lights and lamps and candles in every window. It's a bit like our Advent, the start of the Christian year, which is also celebrated with lights and candles.

> What we call the beginning is often
> the end
> And to make an end is to make a
> beginning.

The end is where we start from . . .

We shall not cease from exploration
And the end of all our exploring
Will be to arrive where we started
And know the place for the first
    time.

T.S. Eliot (1888–1965)
Little Gidding (1942)

19 NOVEMBER
— —

Things have gone from bad to worse in Bosnia, and now the sub-zero winter temperatures are added to the fear and misery that the people are having to endure. But these brave people still hang on in Sarajevo: Muslims, Croats and Serbs, sharing their neighbourhood life. But now they are without electricity or running water, often without anything to eat, where snippers' bullets pock-mark the walls — right inside their homes. What have they done to deserve this? Nothing. They've done nothing to deserve this. It's as though someone has decided to allow all their worst, most violent football hooligans to take charge of the country.

And he shall judge among many
people, and rebuke strong nations
afar off; and they shall beat their
swords into plowshares, and their

spears into pruninghooks: nation
shall not lift up a sword against
nation, neither shall they learn war
any more.
But they shall sit every man under
his vine and under his fig tree; and
none shall make them afraid: for
the mouth of the Lord of hosts has
spoken it.
For all people will walk every one
in the name of his god, and we will
walk in the name of the Lord our
God, for ever and ever.

Micah 4:3–5

20 NOVEMBER

Whenever there's some tragedy — a terrible
accident, or a violent murder, or a bomb in a
public place reported on the news — people
place flowers at the scene, still wrapped up in
paper from the shop. I don't remember people
doing it when I was young. I wonder if it's
something to do with television — people
knowing that the cameras will be there, in their
community, at the place where the terrible
thing happened. I don't mean they are trying 'to
make the place look nice for the cameras' — but
it's as though the flowers are saying, 'It wasn't
the place's fault. The people who live here *do*
care.'

We all need to have ritual in our lives. It helps us to cope with times of celebration and times of tragedy. This flower laying ritual has grown out of people's and communities' need to cope with so much public disaster.

> I got me flowers to strew thy way,
> I got me boughs off many a tree;
> But thou wast up by break of day,
> And brought'st thy sweets along
> with thee.
>
> *George Herbert (1593–1633)*
> *Easter Song*

21 NOVEMBER

O God of many names,
lover of all nations,
we pray for peace
in our hearts,
in our homes,
in our nations,
in our world,
the peace of your will,
the peace of our need.

Bishop George Appleton (d.1993)

22 NOVEMBER

So many television programmes recently have been about the assassination of President John F. Kennedy. This year, 1993, has been the thirtieth anniversary. I said to Scottie the other night, 'What do you want to watch tonight, darling? A documentary about the assassination of President Kennedy, or a programme of people saying what they were doing the day they heard Kennedy had been assassinated, or a dramatic reconstruction of That Day in Dallas, or the memoirs of a friend of Jackie Kennedy?'

I don't mean any disrespect — it *was* a terrible shame. It's just that I don't particularly want to watch endless programmes about it. Life goes on.

> The downy seeds of Travellers Joy
> fill the air, and driving before a gale
> appear like insects on the wing.
> Mrs Clement brought to bed of a
> boy. My nephews and nieces now
> fifty-three . . ..
>
> *Gilbert White*
> *Journals, 1788*

23 NOVEMBER

Although I shall always think of myself as a 'Northerner', in recent years we have come to think of the Sussex Downs almost as our second home. Revd Gilbert White, whose letters and journals I have been quoting from here and there, is an especial favourite of mine because in his day he was a frequent visitor to these parts — and loved it just as much as we do.

> Though I have now travelled the Sussex Downs upwards of thirty years, yet I still investigate that chain of majestic mountains with fresh admiration year by year; and think I see new beauties every time I traverse it. This range, which runs from Chichester eastward as far as Eastbourne, is about sixty miles in length, and is called the South Downs, properly speaking, only round Lewes. As you pass along you command a noble view of the wild, or weald, on one hand, and the broad downs and sea on the other.

> *Gilbert White*
> *Letter to Daines Barrington, 1773*

24 NOVEMBER

I've hardly been able to bear looking at my newspaper recently, because every day there has been page after page about the trial of two ten-year-old children, Child A and Child B, who today have been found guilty of deliberately murdering the little toddler, James Bulger. I don't know how any of the parents are ever going to get over what has happened, but I do know they will all need our prayers if there is ever to be any peace of mind for any of them ever again.

A Father's Prayer upon the Murder of his Son

O God,
We remember not only our son but
also his murderers;
Not because they killed him in the
prime of his youth and made our
hearts bleed and our tears flow,
Not because with this savage act
they have brought further disgrace
on the name of our country among
the civilized nations of the world;
But because through their crime we
now follow thy footsteps more
closely in the way of sacrifice.
The terrible fire of this calamity
burns up all selfishness and
possessiveness in us;
Its flame reveals the depth of
depravity and meanness and
suspicion, the dimension of hatred
and the measure of sinfulness in
human nature;

311

It makes obvious as never before
our need to trust in God's love as
shown in the cross of Jesus and his
resurrection;
Love which makes us free from
hate towards our persecutors;
Love which brings patience,
forbearance, courage, loyalty,
humility, generosity, greatness of
heart;
Love which more than ever deepens
our trust in God's final victory and
his eternal designs for the Church
and for the world;
Love which teaches us how to
prepare ourselves to face our own
day of death.
  O God,
Our son's blood has multiplied the
fruit of the Spirit in the soil of our
souls;
So when his murderers stand before
thee on the day of judgement,
Remember the fruit of the Spirit by
which they have enriched our lives,
And forgive.

Bishop Dehqani–Tafti of Iran

25 NOVEMBER

Thanksgiving — USA

We always celebrate Thanksgiving at our house.
It started when Jan was living in America, and
she would give a big dinner party and raise both
the American flag and the British flag. So it's
become rather a family tradition. William
provides a giant pumpkin from the garden for
the pumpkin soup, which Jan serves from inside
a pumpkin skin. The first time she did it I didn't
know, and I thought, 'What's that pumpkin
doing sitting on the table?'

> We hold these truths to be self-
> evident that all men are created
> equal, that they are endowed by
> their Creator with certain
> inalienable rights, that among these
> are life, liberty and the pursuit of
> happiness.
> *American Declaration of Independence*
> *July 1776*

26 NOVEMBER

Children in Need

Once again, the BBC are doing their Children
in Need appeal all day on the radio and

television. Playing a big part is Mr Blobby — a gigantic pink balloon-man with blobby spots all over him. All he says is 'Blobby, blobby, blobby!' as he rushes about knocking things over and crashing into everybody. This year everyone knows Mr Blobby — but I wonder if, even by the time you read this, in 1994, anyone will remember who he is! It's like one of those old knock-knock jokes:

'Knock, knock.'
'Who's there'
'Mr Blobby'
'Mr Blobby who?'
'That's show business!'

27 NOVEMBER

When Scottie pours the wine at any family gathering we always raise our glasses and drink a toast to 'Absent Friends'.

When our great nephew, Jack Shepherd, was born with a hole in his heart and was so poorly, Scottie and I, who were in Sorrento at the time, added a toast which was really a prayer, 'To Absent Friends — and young Jack Shepherd'. Jack is eighteen months old now and has flourished, but we still often raise our glasses to 'Absent Friends and young Jack Shepherd'!

Lord, give us to go blithely on our
business all this day, bring us to
our resting beds weary and content
and undishonoured, and grant us in
the end the gift of sleep.
        Robert Louis Stevenson (1850–94)

28 NOVEMBER

Here is a poem of really good sense — Rudyard
Kipling's 'The Gods of the Copybook
Headings'.

As I pass through my incarnations in
    every age and race,
I make my proper prostrations to the
    Gods of the Market-Place.
Peering through reverent fingers I
    watch them flourish and fall,
And the Gods of the Copybook
    Headings, I notice, outlast them all.

We were living in trees when they
    met us. They showed us each in turn
That water would certainly wet us, as
    fire would certainly burn:
But we found them lacking in uplift,
    vision and breadth of mind,
So we left them to teach the
    gorillas while we followed the march
    of Mankind . . .

. . . Then the Gods of the Market
    tumbled, and their smooth-tongued
    wizards withdrew,
And the hearts of the meanest were
    humbled and began to believe it was
    true
That all is not gold that glitters, and
    two and two make four —
And the Gods of the Copybook
    Headings limped up to explain it
    once more.

Rudyard Kipling (1865–1936)

29 NOVEMBER

This has been a day I shall never forget. Daisy
and James flew over from Los Angeles to come
with their mother and me to see the Queen!
('We haven't any money, but we do see life!' as
the old song goes.)

Her Majesty presented me with my Dame
insignia. There were quite a few of us there
receiving awards, including George Bush, but
I was 'on' first. I wondered a bit about that, but
the man said, 'It's not like a theatre here. It's all
right to be on first.'

Jan and Daisy and James were watching,
bursting with pride, as I went up and did my
courtsey. They even give you a video of it at the
end! Afterwards we all went home to tell Scottie
all about it, and have the sandwiches he had

prepared for us, and catch up with all the family news, before getting ready to go out to the Royal Lancaster for the party we gave for friends in the evening. And you can guess what everyone said to me as they arrived, can't you?

There is nothin' like a dame!
Oscar Hammerstein II (1895–1960)

30 NOVEMBER

St Andrew's Day

The Church of Scotland is international, and at St Andrew's-tide, their patron saint, they will be holding services and marches with bagpipes all over the world. If you live a long way south of Scotland, but could get to St Columba's, Pont Street in London, for instance, you will find yourself sharing in a deeply impressive service. They take pride in being the People of the Book, so more than hymns they love to sing the psalms. One of the finest is the metrical setting of Psalm 24, 'Ye Gates'. The Hallelujahs and the Amens at the end go on for ever — it's great!

Ye gates, lift up your heads on
    high;
  ye doors that last for aye,
Be lifted up, that so the King
  of glory enter may.

But who of glory is the King?
The mighty Lord is this;
Ev'n that same Lord, that great in
    might
    and strong in battle is.

Ye gates, lift up your heads; ye
    doors
    doors that do last for aye,
Be lifted up, that so the King
    of glory enter may.
But who is he that is the King
    of glory? Who is this?
The Lord of hosts, and none but
    he,
    the King of glory is.
Hallelujah! Hallelujah! Hallelujah! .
    . .
Amen! Amen! Amen!

arr. *Andrew Mitchell Thomson*
(1778–1831)

DECEMBER

I can never remember whether it snowed for six days and six nights when I was twelve or whether it snowed for twelve days and twelve nights when I was six.

Dylan Thomas (1914–53)
A Child's Christmas in Wales

1 DECEMBER

It *can't* be December already! The older you get, the shorter the time seems to be from one Christmas to the next. I swear that if I live long enough, life will be all one long Christmas Day! I love Christmas — so I won't mind a bit.

I'm always very busy in December, because I'm lucky enough to be invited to lots of different Christmas carol services, and there's nothing I enjoy more. The old, old story loses none of its wonder and charm, however many times you hear it.

> I am Gabriel. I stand in the
> presence of God, and I have been
> sent to speak to you and to tell you
> this good news.
>
> *Luke 1:19 (NIV)*

2 DECEMBER

Christians must prepare themselves spiritually for Christmas, and not just by rushing around shopping for presents, writing and posting cards, or cooking mince pies, puddings and cakes! In church, during Advent, candles are lit on an Advent wreath to count us through the four Sundays in December. Some vicars let a young member of the congregation or a choirboy or girl come to the front and light it.

It's right to let the young help us prepare for the future, isn't it? After all, they'll *be* the Church when we are playing our harps!

> I will send my messenger ahead of you,
> who will prepare your way —
> a voice of one calling in the desert,
> 'Prepare the way for the Lord,
> make straight paths for him.'
>
> *Mark 1:2–3 (NIV)*

3 DECEMBER

There's an old Advent carol that you don't hear very often these days — but the words are great.

> 'Tis ill for a mind to anger inclined
> To think of small injuries now;
> If wrath be to seek, do not lend her
>   thy cheek,
> Nor let her inhabit thy brow.
> Cross out of thy books malevolent
>   looks,
> Both beauty and youth's decay,
> And wholly consort with mirth and
>   with sport
> To drive the cold winter away!
>
> This time of the year is spent in
>   good cheer,

And neighbours together do meet,
To sit by the fire, with friendly
    desire,
Each other in love to greet.
Old grudges forgot are put in the
    pot,
All sorrows aside they lay;
The old and the young doth carol
    this song,
To drive the cold winter away.

T. Durfey (1653–1723)
'All Hail to the Days'

4 DECEMBER

One thing I'll miss this year is going down to
the cottage for the Christingle service in the
village church at the beginning of December.
It's beautiful!

During the service all the youngest children
come to the front and are each given an orange,
tied round with a red ribbon, with four cocktail
sticks full of dried fruit — sultanas and raisins
and things — sticking out. On top of each
orange is a lighted candle, so as the children
process round the church with their
'Christingles', we all hold our breath, in case
anyone sets fire to the hair of the person in
front!

It's rounded like an orange,
This earth on which we stand
And we praise the God who holds it
In the hollow of his hand.

A candle burning brightly
Can cheer the darkest night,
And these candles tell how Jesus
Came to bring a dark world light.

The ribbon round the orange
Reminds us of the cost;
How the Shepherd, strong and gentle,
Gave his life to save the lost.

Four seasons with their harvest
Supply the food we need,
And the Spirit gives a harvest
That can make us rich indeed.

We come with our Christingles
To tell of Jesus' birth
And we praise the God who blessed
us
By his coming to this earth.

So, Father, we would thank you,
For all that you have done,
And for all that you have given us,
Through the coming of your Son.

Basil Bridge
Especially written for Christingle services
in aid of the Church of England
Children's Society

5 DECEMBER

The postman delivers a pile of Christmas cards every morning now, and with no cottage to hang them up in (on long strings along the corridors), the mews is going to have to cope with the lot! I love reading the loving messages, but please don't misunderstand me when I admit that I'm finding writing them and sending them increasingly tiring.

And the expense is shocking! I said to Scottie, I think that next year we should only send cards to our old friends who we still love but no longer see very often. It does seem a bit silly — sending them to people you see nearly every day, and have probably wished 'A Happy Christmas' to at least a dozen times already!

> The only cards that really count
> Are that extremely small amount
> From real friends who keep in touch
> And are not rich but love us much.
>
> *John Betjeman*
> *Advent 1955*

6 DECEMBER

St Nicholas

How old were you when you stopped believing in Santa Claus? If you were lucky you will have had the excitement of going to bed on Christmas Eve, leaving a stocking at the end of your bed, in the full belief that a mysterious, magical old man with a flowing white beard would squeeze himself down the chimney and fill your stocking with little presents — right up until you were eight or nine years old!

St Nicholas became the patron saint of children because he rescued three children who were being pickled in a brine tub. Many children today are still being pickled in brine tubs — television and video-game brine tubs! So if you can — rescue a few today!

Simple Gifts

'Tis the gift to be simple, 'tis the gift
   to be free,
'Tis the gift to come down where you
   ought to be,
And when we find ourselves in the
   place just right,
'Twill be in the valley of love and
   delight.

When true simplicity is gained,
To bow and to bend we shan't be
   ashamed;
To turn, turn will be our delight,
Till by turning, turning we come
   round right.

Shaker song
American (1837–47)

7 DECEMBER

Another kind of gift is to be able to live your life one day at a time. It's one thing to enjoy your happy memories, quite another to spend today in pointless regrets. It's good to look forward to the future but not if it spoils today by filling you with worry and alarm.

Do you know this little rhyme?

> Yesterday's history
> Tomorrow's a mystery
> Today is a gift —
> That is why it is called
>   'The Present'
>
> *Anon*

8 DECEMBER

Life is so hard for wild creatures in the winter. Out in the windy, frozen fields you'll see hares crouched in one spot all day, a picture of silent, patient endurance.

> While I watch the Christmas blaze
> Paint the room with ruddy rays,
> Something makes my vision glide
> To the frostly scene outside.

There, to reach a rotting berry,
Toils a thrush — constrained to very
Dregs of food by sharp distress,
Taking such with thankfulness.

Why, O starving bird, when I
One day's joy would justify,
And put misery out of view,
Do you make me notice you?
Thomas Hardy
The Reminder

9 DECEMBER

Going into the garden to put out food for the
birds at this time of year, we've sometimes
discovered fresh molehills in a long line across
the grass. If you squash them, half an hour later
you may see an indignant little head appear in
one of them, and the earthy hills reappear one
by one, and twice the size they were before you
knocked 'em flat!

Loving means to love the unlovable,
or it is no virtue at all; forgiving
means to pardon the unpardonable,
or it is no virtue at all; faith means

328

believing the unbelievable, or it is
no virtue at all; and to hope means
hoping when things are hopeless,
or it is no virtue at all.
                                        G.K. Chesterton

10 DECEMBER

I know it can be a nuisance to have a few
hundred yards of tunnelling under your lawn,
interspersed with mounds of earth — but I've
always felt rather honoured whenever we have
had a mole family busily living their lives in our
garden. I only wish I could have little windows
in the lawn, like a glass-bottomed boat, so I
could see what they were doing down there!

Praise to the Holiest in the height,
And in the depth be praise:
In all his words most wonderful,
Most sure in all his ways.
                    Cardinal J.H. Newman (1801–90)

11 DECEMBER

Scottie and I love to go to Whitelys — a big
shopping precinct just five minutes' walk from
the mews. It's fascinating to sit in one of the
cafes or restaurants, watching the world go by.
In Whitelys these days 'the world' mostly

comes dressed in long flowing Arab robes, the
women's faces hidden behind yashmaks . . ..
They remind us of the Three Wise Men, who
came from the east following a star!

> My fiftieth year had come and
> gone,
> I sat, a solitary man
> In a crowded London shop,
> An open book and empty cup
> On the marble table-top.
>
> While on the shop and street I
> gazed
> My body of a sudden blazed;
> And twenty minutes more or less
> It seemed, so great my happiness,
> That I was bless'd and I could
> bless.

> *W.B. Yeats (1865–1939)*
> *Vacillation*

12 DECEMBER
--

An Advent haiku.

> Young angels and kings
> Not used to haloes and crowns
> Held by safety-pins.

> *Laurence Smith*

13 DECEMBER

Daisy, our granddaughter, was born in America on 13 December, but over here, because of the time difference, it was already 14 December, Jan's own birthday. So when she telephoned us from her hospital bed to say that Daisy had arrived safely, the first thing Scottie and I said to her was 'Happy birthday, darling!'

Doesn't it make Christmas special if there's a new baby in the family? I'll never forget listening to the church bells on Christmas morning with my new baby, Jan, in my arms. Mary, preparing for the birth of her baby, was full of hopes and dreams for a better world that every mother has when she thinks about the future of her children.

Magnificat
My soul doth magnify the Lord.
And my spirit hath rejoiced in God
my Saviour.
For he hath regarded the low estate
of his handmaiden:
for, behold, from henceforth all
generations shall call me blessed.
For he that is mighty hath done to
me great things; and holy is his name.
And his mercy is on them that fear
him from generation to generation.
He hath shewed strength with his
arm; he hath scattered the proud in

the imagination of their hearts.
He hath put down the mighty from
their seats, and exalted them of low
degree.
He hath filled the hungry with
good things; and the rich he hath
sent empty away.

Luke 1:46–53

14 DECEMBER

There's a lovely time, early in the morning
before you are properly awake, when you lie in
bed still half in your dreams. Almost as soon as
you become aware of it, the happy, weightless
feeling starts to disappear and your body
remembers all its aches and pains, and reality
comes surging back. But for a few seconds, it's
like a brief foretaste of heaven.

. . . the dayspring from on high
hath visited us, To give light to
them that sit in darkness and in the
shadow of death, to guide our feet
into the way of peace.

Luke 1:78–79

Here's part of a story in a beautiful little book of Christmas stories and poems by — now I bet this will surprise you — Agatha Christie Mallowan, *the* Agatha Christie, writing under her married name. 'The Island' is a story which imagines the life of Jesus' mother, Mary, now an old lady, long after the crucifixion, living with St John on the island of Patmos.

The moon rose in the sky, and it made a silvery path across the water, and as the light grew stronger, Mary saw a boat approaching. She thought, 'The strangers are coming back again . . .' But it was not the strangers . . . She could see now that it was not the handsome carved boat of the strangers. This was a rough fishing boat — the kind of boat that had been familiar to her all her life . . .

And then she knew — quite certainly . . . . It was *his* boat, and he had come for her at last . . ..

And she ran, slipping and stumbling over the rough stones of the beach. And as she reached the water's edge, half sobbing and half panting, she saw one of the three men step out of the boat onto the sea and walk along the moonlit path towards

her. Nearer and nearer he came . . .
and then — and then . . . she was
clasped in his arms . . .

Words poured from her,
incoherently, trying to tell so much. 'I
have done as you asked me — I have
looked after John — he has been as a
son to me. I am not clever — I cannot
always understand his high thoughts
and his visions, but I have made him
good food, and washed his feet, and
tended him and loved him . . .. I have
been his mother, and he has been my
son . . .?' She looked anxiously up
into his face, asking him a question.

'You have done all I asked you,' he
said gently. 'Now — you are coming
home with me.'

Agatha Christie Mallowan
Star over Bethlehem

16 DECEMBER

Time to think, as we do our chores in the
kitchen, of our dear friend Dr John Tudor, the
minister in charge of the Methodist Central
Hall, Westminster. I know Christmas is always
such a very busy time for John and his team,
providing lunch for hundreds of homeless
people who will turn up on Christmas Day.

A cry in the night
And a child is born;
A child in a stable,
There isn't any room:
A cry in the night, and God has made
Our homelessness his home.

Geoff Ainger (b. 1925)
Ballad of the Homeless Christ

17 DECEMBER

Wesley's Chapel in London has also become a regular port of call for me in recent years, to join in their carol service. They always give me my favourite 'Christmas present' — a Salvation Army band leading the congregation in 'While shepherds watched their flocks by night' to the tune 'Lyngham' — which I remember from Christmas mornings in Cheapside. It was always the Morecambe Borough Band's opening number and, in my humble opinion, is far the best tune to sing it to — and it gives the fellers a chance to show off!

While shepherds watched their flocks
   by night,
All seated on the ground,
All sea-ea-eated on the ground,
The angel of the Lord came down,
And glory shone around,
And glory shone around,

335

And glo-o-o-ory shone around!
Nathum Tate (1652–1715)

18 DECEMBER

A year or two ago, at a church in Nottingham, I was at *their* Carolthon, but when I went to ascend the eight steps up into the pulpit, the round ball on the top of the ballustrade — you know, that you can hold onto to pull yourself up with — was so highly polished, my hand slipped and the next minute I had disappeared from view!

So at Wesley's Chapel, this year, when I had got up into their pulpit — which is the one John Wesley himself used to preach from, by the way — I said, 'This is an achievement! I'm the Queen of falling down and disappearing — but here I am!' They laughed so warmly, I used a very old music hall gag and went on: 'My dear friends — I do not call you "ladies and gentlemen" because I know you too well!' I wasn't sure how they would take it — but everyone laughed so much, I needn't have worried.

It's such a joy for me to spend the days before Christmas surrounded by so much love.

How silently, how silently,
The wondrous gift is given!
So God, imparts to human hearts
The blessings of his heaven.

No ear may hear his coming;
But in this world of sin,
Where meek souls will receive him, still
The dear Christ enters in.
Bishop Phillips Brooks (1835–93)
'O Little Town of Bethlehem'

19 DECEMBER

What do you do when your vicar announces,
'We shall now sing hymn 108 — verses one to
three, and verses five to eight, *omitting* verse
four'? I can't help it — I always have to look
closely at verse four to see why we aren't singing
it! Is it because the theology is thought to be too
sensational for the average congregation . . . or
what? The following verse is nearly always
omitted from the carol 'O Little Town of
Bethlehem' and I think it's a shame, because I
like it — so I'm giving it 'a day' all to itself!

Where children pure and happy
Pray to the blessed child,
Where misery cries out to thee,
Son of the mother mild;
Where charity stands watching
And faith holds wide the door,
The dark night wakes, the glory
   breaks,
And Christmas comes once more.
Bishop Phillips Brooks (1835–93)
'O Little Town of Bethlehem'

I was looking out of the window during a very cold spell and I saw something on the path that I thought was a bird, then I thought it was a leaf. Then I thought, no, it is a bird, and then I thought, no, it is a leaf. The more I looked at it, the more I couldn't decide whether it was a bird or a leaf, so in the end I put on my coat and hat and furry boots and went outside to investigate.

It was a bird, a little sparrow, with his feathers all puffed out to keep him warm. But something was the matter, because I was able to walk right up to him, and bend down and pick him up, and he didn't move or struggle. He was alive, though, because he looked at me with a pair of bright eyes.

I looked him over very gently to see if he was injured, but I couldn't see anything. I carried him carefully back indoors, thinking I would find a little box to put him in. But I was wondering what I was going to do with him after that because, to be honest, I couldn't see Scottie and me spending Christmas going in and out of the garden to dig for worms, and I didn't know what the vet would say if I brought him a sparrow to look after!

I said a little prayer.

Lord, your Holy Spirit flies over the face of all the earth. If it is possible, let this little sparrow fly again, too.

And the little bird started to struggle in my hands. I carried him to the garden door, opened my hands, and away he flew as though nothing had ever been the matter with him.

Just another good gift from God, one of so many for which I am so very grateful.

21 DECEMBER

— —

Today is the shortest day of the year. After today, every day will seem that little bit longer and lighter. It's a nice idea to go out today and bring holly and ivy and mistletoe into the house, just like our pagan ancestors always did. The greenery bearing their berries and fruit when the rest of nature seems dead are like a promise that life goes on — even on our shortest, coldest, darkest days.

There is heard a hymn when the
    panes are dim,
And never before or again,
When the nights are strong and a
    darkness long,
And the dark is alive with the rain.

Never we know but in sleet and in
    snow,
The place where the great fires are,

That the midst of the earth is a raging
  mirth
And the heart of the earth is a star.

And at night we win to the ancient
  inn
Where the child in the frost is furled,
We follow the feet where all souls
  meet
At the inn at the end of the world.

The gods lie dead where the leaves lie
  red,
For the flame of the sun is flown,
The gods lie cold where the leaves lie
  gold,
And a child comes forth alone.
                    G.K. Chesterton (1874–1936)

22 DECEMBER
- -

I always look forward to the carol singers
coming. Sometimes we miss them, if we're
away, and I think some years they just don't
come any more. They may be rarer in towns and
cities, but I don't think the custom will ever die
out in country villages.

In the fore-court, lit by the dim rays
of a horn lantern, some eight or ten
little field mice stood in a semi-circle,
red worsted comforters round their

throats, their forepaws thrust deep into their pockets, their feet jiggling for warmth. With bright beady eyes they glanced slowly at each other, sniggering a little, sniffing and applying coat-sleeves a good deal. As the door opened, one of the elder ones that carried the lantern was just saying, 'Now then, one, two, three!' and forthwith their shrill little voices uprose on the air, singing one of the old-time carols that their fore-fathers composed in fields that were fallow and held by frost, or when snowbound in chimney corners, and handed down to be sung in the miry street of lamp-lit windows at Yuletime.

Kenneth Grahame (1859–1932)
The Wind in the Willows

23 DECEMBER

This year, the year I'm writing this, Scottie and I will be going down to Chichester to spend Christmas with Jan and William in their new home. Daisy and James will be in America. It will seem strange without them, but we'll talk to them on the telephone on Christmas Day.

We'll listen to the Festival of Nine Lessons and Carols from Kings on the radio on

Christmas Eve, while we put the finishing touches to the tree. Jan and I will probably both blub when the little boy starts to sing the first verse of 'Once in royal David's city' as a solo, remembering Daisy doing it when she was still at Benenden, at her end-of-term carol concert.

> Once in royal David's city
> Stood a lowly cattle shed,
> Where a mother laid her baby
> In a manger for his bed:
> Mary was that mother mild
> Jesus Christ her little child.
>
> *C.F. Alexander (1818–95)*

24 DECEMBER

Christmas Eve

The Oxen

Christmas Eve, and twelve of the
   clock.
'Now they are all on their knees',
An elder said, as we sat in a flock,
By the embers in fireside ease.

We pictured the meek mild creatures,
   where
They dwelt in their strawy pen,
Nor did it occur to one of us there
To doubt they were kneeling then.

So fair a fancy few would weave
In these years! Yet, I feel
If someone said, on Christmas Eve,
'Come, see the oxen kneel.

'In the lonely barton by yonder
    coomb,
Our childhood used to know',
I should go with him in the gloom,
Hoping it might be so.

Thomas Hardy

25 DECEMBER

Christmas Day

Christmas morning at Cheapside always began
in the same way. We were awakened by the
Salvation Army band, who were standing in the
middle of the road, and musically demanding
that 'Christians Awake! Salute this Happy
Morn!' Everyone, Christian or not, awoke, and
as Cheapside was such a happy street, we
saluted the happy morn without any trouble.

We all had stockings in our house, and the
annual Christmas morning joke, and always a
'sure laugh', was when Father unpacked his
stocking and feigned surprise when he
discovered an onion, a potato and a carrot
instead of the expected apple and orange, etc!

Parents try to make their children's wishes

come true at Christmas. I remember the card my mother put with a beautiful little watch that I had set my heart on and tried to save for, but was sure I would never have, yet which I found in a little jeweller's box in the toe of my stocking one Christmas morning. It read:

> Just to fulfil one desire, I wish I could fulfil them all! Mother

26 DECEMBER

St Stephen's Day

I enjoy our family meal on Boxing Day almost as much, if not more, than the real Christmas Day lunch. We put everything out on the big table — cold turkey, all the different stuffings and sauces, a big, home-cured ham, mince pies — the lot! And then it's every man — or woman — for themself!

> In a sometimes lonely,
> somewhere hungry world,
> for food and friendship
> we give you thanks, good Lord.
> *Unitarian grace*

27 DECEMBER

In London after Christmas you always get the great New Clothes Parades in the parks! Families go out together, and they are all wearing their new Christmas pullovers — even staid old businessmen! I love it. And another thing I love about this time of year is the smell of damp wool — mittens and scarves gently steaming on the radiators after wet or snowy afternoon perambulations!

> Glory to God in the highest,
> and on earth peace among men
> in whom he is well pleased.
>
> *Luke 2:14*

28 DECEMBER

Holy Innocents

The shops and the media talk about Christmas as though it were a time of unbounded joy — but that's neither Christian nor realistic. The real Christmas story is a dark one, as much about fear and homelessness, danger and death, as it is about birth and hope. The terrible stories we've been hearing and reading in the press about tiny children, no more than babies some of them, found alone in freezing cold houses with no food, are a stark reminder that the world Jesus was born into and came to save is still a dark, cold and often wicked one.

> In Rama was there a voice heard, lamentation, and weeping, and great mourning, Rachel weeping for her children, and would not be comforted, because they are not.
>
> *Matthew 2:18*

29 DECEMBER

I do enjoy these quiet days between Christmas and the New Year, when there's a little bit of free time, and the pressure of the next bit of work hasn't started yet. I even enjoy writing my 'thank you letters' for all the gifts and kind thoughts we've received over Christmas.

> He hath shewed thee, O man, what is good; and what doth the Lord require of thee, but to do justly, and to love mercy, and to walk humbly with thy God?
>
> *Micah 6:8*

30 DECEMBER

Being in the depth of winter, I suppose it's not very surprising that a lot of people seem to fall ill over Christmas. I find the end of December is often a time for visiting friends in hospital. Here is another of those beautiful Plain Man's prayers by William Barclay.

O God,
At the beginning of the year I never
thought that at the end of it I would
be here in this place. It is just as well
that we cannot see in advance what is
going to happen to us.
Thank you,
    for everything that has happened
this year.
Thank you,
    for the things which will always be
happy memories.
Thank you,
    for the things which showed me
my own weakness,
    and which kept me humble.
Thank you,
    for the things which compelled me
to remember you,
    and to realize how much I need
you.
Thank you,
    for the loyalty of friends and the
faithfulness
    of loved ones.
Thank you
    even for this illness,

which has shown me how kind
people can be;
   which has made me appreciate the
skill of doctors
   and the devotion of nurses;
   and which has made me realize
what a gift
   good health is.
Hear this my prayer, for your love's
sake. Amen.

William Barclay

31 DECEMBER

New Year's Eve

Well, if you want to know, we'll probably be
spending it quietly on our own, and we may
even get to bed before midnight! But Scottie
and I wish you all a very loving and happy new
year, full of happy days.

Pray for me, as I will pray for you,
until the day we all meet merrily in
heaven.

ACKNOWLEDGEMENTS

The author and publisher acknowledge with thanks permission to use the material quoted in this book.

Thora Hird:
I Believe: Stories of faith
from *Saga*

Thora Hird, like many other people, is an
avid reader of *Saga* Magazine. In fact, more
than half a million copies of the magazine go
out to the homes of older people in Britain
ten times a year.

One of the most lively pages of the magazine
is the letters page, with its exchange of
stories, views and ideas about everything
under the sun.

A regular feature of the letters page has been
the 'I Believe' column, in which a reader
reflects on his or her faith and the spiritual
side of life. Although only one can be
included in each issue of the magazine, the
editor has received many hundreds of letters.

Now Thora Hird has compiled a selection of
these letters with her own introduction and
personal reflections. It is an inspiring and
moving addition to her best-selling series of
Praise Be! books.

Thora Hird's
Christmas Book

Thora Hird's Praise Be! Christmas Book is "a bit like an Advent Calendar", with thoughts, prayers, recipes, carols and poems for each day of December and a few beyond.

As befits the homespun philosophy of this popular comedy actress, there is nothing very profound about the book's contents, but it could provide a lighter-than-usual devotional guide in the run up to Christmas for those looking for a change.

BAPTIST TIMES

Thora Hird's
Praise Be! Notebook

———

Thora Hird's Praise Be! Notebook is
a selection of the hymns requested by
listeners to the programme that is presented
by Thora Hird. Listed alphabetically, each
section also includes thoughts and ideas that
have gone into the making of the
programme over the years. A book I think a
lot of people might enjoy

EUROPEAN CHRISTIAN BOOKSELLER

Thora Hird's
Praise Be! Prayer Book

Viewers of the popular BBC television programme, *Praise Be!*, presented by Thora Hird, will need little encouragement to buy her latest book.

She has collected together favourite prayers (a delightful mixture of old and new) and interspersed them with touching and amusing anecdotes from her own experience.

She chats as easily with the written word as she does with the spoken word on television. All this goes to make up a super little book to buy for yourself or to give to a friend.

CHRISTIAN HERALD

❋

For 15 years a regular five million viewers have made *Praise Be!* one of Britain's best loved television programmes. And there is no secret to its success – presenter Thora Hird lets all the viewers know they are special, but that their moments of sadness and joy are shared by many others.

In *Praise Be! Prayer Book* she has collected her favourites – old and new, written by the famous and the forgotten and even some sent by viewers. It is a book that cannot fail to bring comfort in times of trouble and help the reader to give thanks for blessings in times of joy.

METHODIST RECORDER

Thora Hird's
Praise Be! Yearbook

A delightful book, you can dip into Thora
Hird's *Praise Be!* selections or read them
straight through. Thora writes as she talks,
you can hear her rich North Country tones
coming through – with shades of "Last of
the Summer Wine"!

There are lots of letters, anecdotes, poetry
and Bible quotations, as well as the words of
favourite hymns and songs – not all old ones
either, *Shine Jesus Shine* is included – all set
out as she moves through the year, taking in
various Christian Festivals, family birthdays
and anniversaries.

A lovely gift for your favourite OAP – or
anyone else who is a *Praise Be!* fan.

CHRISTIAN FAMILY

Thora Hird's
Little Book of Home Truths

———

"I've realized that I am one of those lucky
people who received a double blessing when
I was born: first to grow up in the North of
England, and second, to have had two of the
best and wisest parents in the world.

"This book is a collection of things I
was taught as I was growing up in
Morecambe. And some of them are things
I've learned for myself over eighty years. I
don't suppose they are going to shake the
world – but who knows? The may make life a
little happier for someone."

DAME THORA HIRD